Role
Transitions
in Later Life

BROOKS/COLE SERIES IN SOCIAL GERONTOLOGY

Vern Bengtson, *University of Southern California*
Series Editor

HEALTH AND AGING
Tom Hickey, *University of Michigan*

ENVIRONMENT AND AGING
M. Powell Lawton, *Philadelphia Geriatric Center*

LAST CHAPTERS: A SOCIOLOGY OF AGING AND DYING
Victor W. Marshall, *University of Toronto and McMaster University*

AGING AND RETIREMENT
Anne Foner, *Rutgers University*
Karen Schwab, *Social Security Administration, Washington, D.C.*

ROLE TRANSITIONS IN LATER LIFE
Linda K. George, *Duke University Medical Center*

STRATIFICATION AMONG THE AGED
James J. Dowd, *University of Georgia*

Role Transitions in Later Life

Linda K. George
Duke University Medical Center

Brooks/Cole Publishing Company
Monterey, California
A Division of Wadsworth, Inc.

Printed in the United States of America

10 9 8 7 6 5 4 3 2 1

Library of Congress Cataloging in Publication Data

George, Linda K
   Role transitions in later life.

   (Brooks/Cole series in social gerontology)
   Includes bibliographical references and indexes.
   1. Aged—Psychology.   2. Life cycle, Human.
3. Social adjustment.   I. Title. II. Series.
HQ1061.G39   301.43'5   79-25239
ISBN   0-8185-0382-3

Acquisition Editor: *Todd Lueders*
Production Editor: *Robert Rowland*
Series Design: *John Edeen*
Illustrations: *Ayxa Art*
Typesetting: *Graphic Typesetting Service*

To my grandmother,
Frances Frei Hafely,
and in memory of my grandfather,
Lewis J. Hafely.

Foreword

Stress is a frequent companion to change in the day-to-day business of ordinary living. And change is an inevitable, normal consequence of ordinary human aging.

This book focuses on the expectable transitions of later adulthood—changes in interpersonal networks with the passage of time, and adaptations commonly made by individuals in meeting those alterations. Dr. Linda George, a social psychologist and Assistant Professor of Medical Sociology at the Duke University Center for Human Development and Aging, brings an exceptional array of research experience and conceptual skills to the complex task of analyzing role transitions and stress. The research she reviews reminds us that, in each major transition of aging—retirement from work, widowhood, loss of active parental roles, and residential relocation—there are elements of serious social stress that can threaten happiness and jeopardize psychological well-being.

One of the important contributions of this book is the general model of adjustment to transitional stress that Dr. George presents. The model, derived from her integration of the existing research on social transitions and aging, summarizes current knowledge and points to needed areas of future inquiry. Students, practitioners, and researchers who are interested in understanding personal change and its consequences in the normal transitions of aging will find this model useful. It will very likely be the topic of considerable debate—theoretical, practical, and empirical—among professional gerontologists in the years to come.

An even more intriguing contribution of this volume is found in Dr. George's insistence that even stressful transitions of later life need not inevitably lead to negative consequences for the individual. Aging involves losses that require adaptation, but it's important to realize that the changes of aging can bring opportunity as well as challenge—freedom as well as decrement.

The evidence Dr. George reviews suggests that the majority of older people construct quite successful adaptations to transitional stress. She notes that they adequately negotiate environmental demands, report relatively high levels of life satisfaction, and maintain a meaningful sense of personal identity. Elderly individuals cope. How they cope, and the impact of various conditioning variables that influence the process of adjustment, are described in Dr. George's application of the social stress model to the normal social transitions of later life.

This book is one in a series of monographs concerning social aspects of aging presented by Brooks/Cole Publishing Company. Along with the other volumes in the series, it examines relevant research reflecting three undergirding themes in the relatively young scientific specialty of social gerontology.

The first theme concerns the need to study aging as an interface between person and society, examining aging individuals as they negotiate the changing course of their own developing biography and analyzing the population of older (and younger) people as they portray common transitions and stresses. Therefore, it is necessary, as Dr. George points out, to employ two levels of analysis in examining transitions: one macro-social, focusing on populations, and the other individual social-psychological.

The second theme of the books in this series concerns the role of history and culture in the analysis of behavioral aging. Today's aged are unique; they are, in a sense, pioneers, for never before in history have so many humans lived so long. This is precisely why the transitions Dr. George describes are "expectable" and "normal" to a magnitude that has outstripped our present cultural experience with aging. This also gives us a reason to suspect our commonly held beliefs (perhaps "myths") about the transitions and stresses of aging. By examining other cultures and other historical periods, we are able to penetrate our own ethnocentric expectations concerning what aging "should" be like. Therefore, the comparative perspective is both valuable and necessary in understanding aging.

The third, and related, theme concerns the interplay between continuity and change as we examine human aging. How we negotiate the changes of tomorrow is in part forecast by what we are today, as suggested by Dr. George's model of transitional stress.

This is an important book that should receive a good deal of attention from those who are interested in understanding age-related social transitions and personal stress. Readers will find Dr. George's presentation personally relevant as well as intellectually enlightening. When we come to understand the aging of others today, we might be able to foresee our own transitions and stresses.

Vern L. Bengtson
Series Editor

Preface

My grandmother is 90 years old. During her lifetime, she has witnessed two major world wars, two "skirmishes" in the Far East, and the Great Depression. She has lived her life in the context of industrial growth, urbanization, and technological advances unparalled in the history of civilization. On a personal level, my grandmother married, raised four children, moved from a farm to live in a city, worked outside her home and retired from that work, outlived her brother and sisters, one of her children, and her husband, and adapted splendidly to living alone. In spite of the personal and social changes she has experienced, my grandmother remains unchanged in my eyes. For as long as I can remember, she has been a gentle, contented woman who has brought cheer to others and found fulfillment in hard work, religious devotion, and warm relationships with her friends and family.

My grandmother is very special to me, but she is not unique in her ability to adapt to change and maintain a solid sense of personal well-being. Although their personal histories differ, many of my grandmother's age peers have found equal measures of contentment in spite of the challenges posed by personal and social change. Many other older people, of course, have not fared so well; for them, change has resulted in decreased personal well-being.

The purpose of Role Transitions in Later Life is to explore the types of challenges and transitions commonly encountered during later life and to trace their consequences. In this book, I've attempted to assess the older population as a whole—to identify the most common transitions experienced by older people and examine the typical impact of such transitions on personal well-being. I've also explored the factors that generate individual differences and variant behavior patterns among older individuals in an effort to understand why some older persons successfully negotiate the challenges of change, while others are unable to take them in stride. I believe that it is important to understand the factors that facilitate effective adjustment to change as well as the circumstances that are likely to impede successful adjustment. Although a personal example has been used to introduce the topic, the contents of this book are guided by social science theory—more specifically, a social stress perspective—and by a large body of empirical research findings.

This book contains eight chapters. The first four chapters introduce the concepts and develop the model that will be used to better understand the nature and consequences of stressful role transitions in later life.

Chapter 1 deals with the concepts of status, role, role transition, and social stress. In Chapter 2, I argue that the consequences of social stress can be identified through an examination of two components of personal well-being—identity and adjustment. In Chapter 3, some of the key factors that influence the process of adjustment to social stress are introduced. I maintain that personal resources, coping skills, and social status significantly influence the impact of potentially stressful transitions. Chapter 4 is devoted to the development of a conceptual model of adjustment to social stress. Five models are reviewed and evaluated, and an integrated model—the social stress model—is proposed. In each of these chapters, the concepts and the social stress model are directly related to the circumstances of later life.

In the second half of the book, the ability of the social stress model to increase our understanding of later life is put to the test. In Chapters 5 through 7, the model is used in conjunction with available research findings to examine the major role transitions in three significant arenas of later life—the world of work, the world of the family, and the residential environment. Chapter 5 is devoted primarily to an examination of the impact of retirement on identity and adjustment. Two other work-related experiences of later life also are discussed—part-time work and the return to full-time work after retirement. A number of family-based transitions are examined in Chapter 6: the departure of the last child from the home, the effects of becoming a grandparent, widowhood, and remarriage in later life. Chapter 7 traces the impact of residential relocation and institutionalization on adjustment and identity in later life. Finally, Chapter 8 examines the implications of this examination, emphasizing the general contributions of the social stress perspective. A summary of what is known about the nature and consequences of role transitions in later life is presented in this chapter. Policy and service implications also are reviewed.

One's work inevitably reflects a myriad of factors, including one's personal history, relationships with colleagues, and broad disciplinary traditions. It is impossible to trace the complex effects of these factors or to apportion credit and appreciation in a perfectly equitable manner. I have been most fortunate to profit from the stimulation and relentless rigor of a broad range of colleagues throughout the preparation of this book. I owe a tremendous debt to George L. Maddox, who invariably brings enthusiasm, support, and intellectual rigor to my work. He has been my closest mentor and colleague, and I am very grateful for his many contributions to my career. This book reflects my personal and intellectual debts to James S. House; my work has profited from his intellectual clarity, keen insight, and constructive criticism, and my life has been enriched by his friendship and support.

I wish to thank Mitchell Horwich for bibliographic assistance. Pam Haas and Rosiland E. Thomas typed the manuscript; their efficiency, patience, and good humor are sincerely appreciated.

Vern L. Bengtson deserves special thanks for his numerous contributions to this book. His patience, painstaking devotion to clarity and style, and constant encouragement have been invaluable. Todd Lueders and Bob Rowland of Brooks/Cole Publishing Company have provided essential assistance throughout the preparation of this book. I also wish to express my appreciation to Majda Thurnher, whose extensive and penetrating review of an earlier draft contributed significantly to the final product.

Finally, a special acknowledgment of another sort must be made to my husband, Earl Maynard, for his support of and patience with my occupation and preoccupation during the past few months.

Linda K. George

Contents

Contents

1

Roles, Role Transitions, and Social Stress

Human life is characterized by complex patterns of change and stability—of discontinuity and order. The purpose of this book is to examine some of the changes, or discontinuities, that commonly occur during the second half of adulthood. We will explore the nature of those changes and the ways in which they affect the lives and well-being of middle-aged and older people. This chapter deals with the concepts of **status**[1] and **role** as they are viewed from quite different theoretical perspectives—**structural** and **interactionist.** Then, since statuses and roles are sources of individual change, the dynamics of **role change** are examined. Finally, the concept of **social stress** is discussed.

Status and Role: Structural Perspectives

Classical sociological theories emphasize the utility of objective social structure in predicting and explaining individual and group behavior. Traditionally, the concepts of status and role have been linked to describe positions

[1] Terms that appear in **boldface** are explained in the Glossary at the back of the book.

in the social structure and the behavioral expectations associated with those positions. The classic definitions of *status* and *role* were developed by Ralph Linton (1936):

> A *status*, in the abstract, is a position in a particular pattern. . . . A *role* represents the dynamic aspect of a status. The individual is socially assigned to a status and occupies it with relation to other statuses. When he puts the rights and duties which constitute the status into effect, he is performing a role. Role and status are quite inseparable. . . . There are no roles without statuses or statuses without roles [pp. 113–114].

In other words, a status is a position within a social structure (parent, for example), and a role is the behavioral counterpart of a position (caring for children). By using these concepts, it is possible to identify numerous statuses and to describe the behavioral rights and duties associated with them.

Linton (1936) differentiated **achieved statuses** from **ascribed statuses.** Achieved statuses are those that individuals occupy as a result of their own efforts, motivations, and competence, such as occupational statuses. Ascribed statuses are socially assigned, regardless of the efforts or desires of individuals. Examples of ascribed statuses include gender, race, ethnic-group membership, and family relationships. Ascribed statuses are linked to very basic foundations of social differentiation; consequently, the roles associated with them tend to be broad, diffuse, and difficult to specify.

Status and role are normative phenomena; that is, there are shared definitions of the criteria for occupying particular statuses and the behavior that is expected of those who occupy them. In other words, status and role are normatively-governed entities that are external to the individuals who occupy and enact them. We can identify the status of physician and discuss the rights and responsibilities of physicians without having any particular person in mind.

The statuses individuals occupy define the context in which (and the standards by which) their behavior is evaluated by others. Normative expectations serve as guidelines for behavior, and, because the expectations are shared, the adequacy of one's role performance can be judged. It is commonly acknowledged that parents have a responsibility to care properly for their children and that they have a right to expect a measure of respect and obedience from them in return. Some parents don't care properly for their children; some children do not respect their parents' wishes. In such cases, role performance may be judged inadequate, but the normative expectations regarding proper role performance remain unchanged.

Statuses anchor individuals in the social structure. From the structural perspective, this is viewed as beneficial. People need defined social locations and normative guidelines for behavior. Anomie—a state of normlessness that is presumably uncomfortable—is likely to develop in the absence of structure and behavioral guidelines. Since statuses link individuals to the social structure, they contribute to social integration and personal well-being. On the other hand, it also is true that statuses define duties and impose behavioral constraints on individuals. From the structural perspective, however, the benefits of integration in the social structure outweigh the potential negative consequences of constraint. Structuralists maintain that responsibilities and constraints are in the best interests of both the individual and the larger social system.

In order to perform a role properly, an individual must be aware of the behavioral expectations associated with that role and acquire the knowledge and skills needed to behave in accordance with those expectations. **Socialization** is the process of learning skills and acquiring motivations to appropriately perform roles. Early childhood is a period of intense socialization, during which we learn the basic skills, attitudes, and behaviors that help us to become members of society. During early childhood, we learn language, acquire cultural customs, and develop basic social character—values, morals, and cognitive structures. At this stage, socialization is involuntary (imposed by powerful **significant others**) and tends to occur in highly emotional situations. Although this may seem a grim view of child-rearing, given the emotional attachments between parents and children, childhood is characterized by stringent demands with regard to socialization. This intense process of early social learning is called **primary socialization.**

Individuals acquire and discard a variety of statuses during their lives. As they move in and out of various statuses and social groups, they develop attitudes and skills they need to perform the succession of roles; this is the process of **secondary socialization.** In contrast to primary socialization, secondary socialization involves a narrow scope of skills and attitudes, and it is usually voluntary. The acquisition of occupational skills is an example of secondary socialization.

Inadequate Role Performance

Inadequate role performance can occur in several kinds of situations. Individuals who are aware of behavioral expectations and who possess the skills they need to perform their roles sometimes do not do so. This behavior pattern is an example of deviance as it is conventionally defined. There are no extenuating circumstances. The individual simply ignores behavioral expectations. Not all inadequate role performances reflect indifference to normative expectations. In some cases, socialization is incomplete. In other cases, socialization is complete and successful but inappropriate to actual role demands. Since the socializer is responsible for teaching appropriate behavior, these situations highlight the importance of the socializer in generating successful role performance. Finally, conflicting role expectations sometimes make it impossible for individuals to perform one or more roles appropriately. In some cases, the expectations associated with one role preclude adequate performance of another role.

For example, consider the case of a department store employee (we'll call him Mr. Nelson) who is caught stealing a bicycle from his employer. One possible explanation for this behavior is that Mr. Nelson committed a deviant act: he was aware that his action was illegal, but he chose to steal the merchandise anyway. Another possibility, albeit unlikely, is that he was unaware that his behavior was illegal or that it violated behavioral expectations. A third possibility is that Mr. Nelson's coworkers assured him that a minimal amount of stealing was acceptable on the job—that, indeed, everyone did it and no one was punished. If this was the case, we would say that Mr. Nelson had been socialized by his coworkers but that his behavior was not compatible with the **norms** and **values** of the larger social system. A fourth possibility is that, although Mr. Nelson knew that his behavior violated role expectations, he wanted to give his child a birthday present and couldn't afford to buy one. If this was the case, Mr. Nelson faced conflicting role expectations and chose to perform his parental duties (as he saw them) rather than his employee duties. The important point is that inadequate role performance is not always a reflection of inadequate socialization.

In summary, the traditional sociological perspective emphasizes the structural, objective, and normative qualities of status and role. Socialization is viewed as a process that fosters behavioral conformity by fitting individuals to preexisting social structures and expectations. This structural viewpoint contributes to our understanding of human behavior, but it has limitations. A number of sociologists, particularly those identified with the symbolic interactionist perspective, have suggested balancing the structural tradition with insights from a more subjective viewpoint.

Status and Role: Interactionist Perspectives

According to the traditional view, status and role are structural and objective, and socialization is a process of molding individual behavior to preexisting social expectations. In contrast, interactionist perspectives emphasize individual interpretations of social structure and the ability to affect social structure as well as react to its demands. Interactionists maintain that the individual relates to the social structure through interpretation and social interaction. Although social structure provides the context for behavior, individuals define their relationships to the social structure and help to shape and modify that structure.

The importance of interactionist perspectives in understanding social roles can be seen in three important ways. First, many of us voluntarily and deliberately select the statuses we occupy and the roles we perform. Once we occupy a status, we are subject to a set of behavioral expectations; however, when we remember that we frequently select our statuses, the image of social structure being imposed on individuals loses much of its oppressive connotations.

Second, many roles simply do not have a narrow and rigidly enforced set of behavioral expectations. Instead, adequate role performance often encompasses a wide range of permissible behaviors. Consider, for example, the role of parent. There are duties that must be performed in order to meet parental role requirements; however, beyond these, a wide range of specific behaviors can satisfy the requirements of this role. When a wide range of behaviors constitutes adequate role performance, individuals are affected in two important ways. First, social judgment, or evaluation, of performance ceases to be a straightforward matter. There is "room" for individuals to behave in ways that are compatible with their needs and preferences without fear of social retaliation. Second, individuals often are able to choose the degree to which they meet normative expectations. For example, if a father fails to demonstrate concern for his children, his behavior will be evaluated negatively. If, on the other hand, he demonstrates adequate role performance, the degree to which he lives up to the ideal image of fatherhood is largely his personal decision.

Third, individuals are able to create informal roles that are compatible with their personal preferences and tastes. Unlike formal roles, informal roles aren't associated with a socially assigned status. Ralph Turner (1956) defines role from a symbolic interactionist perspective and specifies two types of roles that may emerge in the absence of socially assigned statuses:

> By *role* we mean a collection of patterns of behavior which are thought to constitute a meaningful unit and deemed appropriate to a person occupying a particular status in society (e.g., doctor or father), occupying an informally defined position in interpersonal relations (e.g., leader or compromisor), or identified with a particular value in society (e.g., honest man or patriot) [p. 316].

When individuals are able to affect social structure, behavior patterns emerge in the absence of socially assigned statuses.

Informal roles don't involve an evaluation of role performance, because they aren't associated with socially assigned statuses and aren't governed by widely shared behavioral expectations. Since such roles exist outside the normative social structure, there are no criteria for evaluating role performance. Informal social roles free individuals in two ways: (1) enactment of roles is largely a matter of personal preference, and (2) social judgment of the adequacy of performance is unlikely.

According to structural perspectives, socialization is a process in which individuals learn to conform to preexisting behavioral expectations. However, since individuals interpret and act on social structure, socialization need not be a straightforward process in which a socializer molds behavior. Interactionists view socialization as a process of negotiation between socializers and others that leads to the development of attitudes, skills, and personal styles that are used in performing roles.

Turner's (1962) distinction between **role-taking** and **role-making** epitomizes the differences between the structuralist and the interactionist views of socialization. Role-taking reflects the structuralist perspective— individuals acquire predefined roles and are socialized to perform those roles. Role-making, on the other hand, reflects the interactionist view—individuals create their own roles, and socialization is the process or set of experiences that leads to the development of roles.

The structuralist and interactionist perspectives are both valuable. The interactionist viewpoint is compatible with the insights provided by the structuralist perspective. Some roles *are* socially defined and normatively governed; however, other roles are informal and emerge through a process of individual initiative and negotiation. The interactionist perspective reminds us to keep sight of the individual's ability to create and modify social structure.

Role Changes and Role Transitions

With the exception of several ascribed statuses (such as gender and race), individuals don't occupy the same statuses and perform the same roles during their entire lives. Instead, the configuration of statuses and roles is continually shifting, requiring life-long negotiation and socialization.

Role shifts can occur in two ways. In some cases, statuses are acquired or discarded, and, as a result, roles are gained or lost. The status of student, for example, is discarded as an individual graduates from school or departs without a degree. In either case, the individual is no longer required or expected to act like a student. (Role shifts that involve the gain or loss of a status will be referred to here as **role transitions**.) In other cases, role expectations change over a period of time. For example, a 10-year-old girl and a 40-year-old woman can both occupy the status of daughter; however, behavioral expectations differ according to the age of the status occupant. The term **role change** will be used here to refer to situations in which status is retained while role expectations change. Role changes often reflect other status or role shifts; for example, the role of daughter changes as the individual moves from the status of child to that of adult. The dynamics of role changes and role transitions highlight issues that are critical to our understanding of socialization and roles.

Some role changes and role transitions are normative. Individuals are expected to alter their behavior and acquire and discard statuses. Students are expected to complete their education and find a suitable occupation. Other role transitions and changes signify a failure to meet normative expectations.

Being fired from a job, for example, is a role transition that results from inadequate role performance. Still other role changes or transitions are normatively irrelevant. Dropping one's membership from the League of Women Voters involves a status and role loss that is unlikely to generate significant public reaction.

Socialization presumably helps individuals to make role changes and transitions smoothly. At times, socialization is formal and relatively intense, but it also can be informal and gradual. In general, role gains involve formal socialization procedures, whereas role losses do not. Formal procedures are used in learning occupational skills, but not in preparing for retirement. Classes are offered for expectant parents, whereas people aren't formally prepared for the departure of children from the parental home. **Anticipatory socialization** refers to socialization that occurs in a gradual way, simply as a consequence of knowing that one will (or may) someday occupy a particular position. Such "mental rehearsals" help prepare the individual for future status occupancy. Recently, a number of popular books have focused on topics such as how to cope with widowhood, how to make divorce a bearable and even an enriching experience, and how to make the most of retirement. Such literature is potentially valuable for informal socialization.

The structural view of status and role logically leads to the conclusion that role gains are beneficial to the individual, whereas role losses are likely to be detrimental. Role gains anchor the individual in the social structure and provide guidelines for social approval. Role losses, on the other hand, break the bonds between the individual and the social structure. Behavior becomes increasingly problematic as guidelines and social rewards become more ambiguous.

The interactionist perspective leads to a less deterministic view of the outcome of role losses and gains. When individuals acquire new roles, the rigidity of the behavioral expectations associated with those roles determines the extent to which the individuals need to conform to sets of predetermined standards of behavior. On the other hand, when behavioral expectations are flexible, the possibilities for role making increase and individuals are able to negotiate their behavior and create behavioral patterns that are compatible with their personal tastes and preferences.

Role changes and role transitions pose potential challenges whether they involve a role-taking process of acquiring the skills, knowledge, and motivations needed to conform to a set of known and accepted social expectations or the negotiations of role-making. Four features of role shifts influence their degree of difficulty: 1) their normative significance, 2) their personal significance, 3) their effect on established patterns of behavior, and 4) the extent to which the individual has been socialized for the role shift.

1. Their normative significance. The more normatively significant the role change or transition, the greater the potential challenge to the individual. Role changes and transitions that are important to society are associated with relatively large rewards and punishments. Failure to achieve or adequately

perform a normatively important role or loss of a socially valued role will lead to disapproval or severe social sanctioning. The acquisition of a valued role leads to social approval and rewards.

2. Their personal significance. The greater the sense of personal loss experienced by the individual, the more difficult the role change or transition will be. Becoming a champion amateur water skiier might appear to be a relatively minor accomplishment to the world at large, but loss of that role might be critical to someone who values that status. In some cases, individuals experience a normatively valued role change or transition as a personal loss. If a worker experiences satisfaction by successfully tackling the repair of complex machines, his or her promotion to a management position might lead to a sense of loss, in spite of the fact that the role transition is socially valued and involves a raise in salary. (A discussion of the personal significance of roles leads directly to issues of personal identity, which are discussed in detail in Chapter 2.)

3. Their effect on established patterns of behavior. Role changes and transitions disrupt established behavior patterns. The degree of difficulty experienced by individuals when they change roles is dependent on the amount of disruption caused by those changes. For example, moving from one community to another is usually more stressful than moving to a different house in the same neighborhood. Although both moves involve change, the former move entails a much greater disruption of customary interactions and routines.

4. The number and nature of socializing experiences individuals have had will affect the impact of role changes and role transitions. Generally, individuals who have had many such experiences are able to deal more successfully with changes and transitions. Of course, some role changes and transitions are so rare that previous experiences provide no clues. Losing one's family to a natural disaster or being held hostage are such rare and catastrophic events that previous socializing experiences are of little help. In other cases, changes and transitions are relatively familiar, but individuals don't expect to experience them personally. For example, we are all aware that there are many persons who experience severe accidents that result in permanent disability, but few of us are psychologically prepared for this possibility. At times, role changes and role transitions occur unexpectedly, precluding socializing experiences that would have occurred at a predictable time. As a result, "early" widowhood may be more difficult to cope with than the loss of a spouse in later life.

In all these cases, the occurrence of unexpected changes and transitions limits socializing experiences. Many people prepare for expected changes and transitions, even though they don't look forward to them. Probably no one wants to die, yet most people make some provisions for death.

Although expected role changes and role transitions offer more opportunities for socialization, the degree to which individuals seek out and participate in socialization varies greatly. Therefore, even the most predictable changes and transitions can be problematic.

Social stress theorists and research investigators are interested in social situations that pose adaptive problems. Stressful social situations are viewed as adaptive challenges that require individual adjustment. Such situations can lead to negative outcomes (illness, mental disorder, and unhappiness, for example). Previous studies of stress have focused on life events—identifiable, discrete changes in life patterns that can create stress. Many of the events examined in the social stress framework involve role changes and role transitions. This provides a direct link between the social stress literature and role theories.

Life events differ in importance and impact. Traditionally, events and situations that involve great amounts of behavioral disruption have been viewed as the most stressful. The conventional social-stress paradigm emphasizes only one aspect of role changes and role transitions—the degree to which they disrupt established patterns of behavior. Some social-stress literature explicitly states that the perception of stress is not an important factor in the impact of stressful events. Both events that are presumably positive, or pleasant (such as marriage), and those that are typically thought of as negative (such as the death of a spouse), are viewed as stressful, because both types of events disrupt established patterns of behavior and require personal adjustment.

The work of Holmes and Rahe and their associates (see Rahe, 1976; Rahe, Meyer, Smith, Kjaer, & Holmes, 1964; Holmes & Rahe, 1967) illustrates the assumptions of traditional social stress theories and the potential interface between social stress and adjustment to role changes and role transitions. In order to investigate the relationship between social stress and health, Holmes and Rahe developed the *Schedule of Recent Events (SRE)*—a checklist of 42 life events that pose challenges to individuals (see Table 1-1). More recently, they developed a 55-item checklist called *The Recent Life Changes Questionnaire (RLCQ)*, which is a modification of the SRE. Most of the life events in both these instruments involve role transitions and role changes.

The SRE and RLCQ illustrate several features of traditional social stress theory. The measures include both positive and negative events. Moreover, both the SRE and the RLCQ include scoring systems that are presumably calibrated to the degree of adjustment required. For example, in the SRE, marriage (presumably a positive event) has a score of 50, while being fired (typically defined as a negative event) is assigned a score of 47. Marriage is seen as having a slightly greater impact on established patterns of behavior. These measures assume that stress is cumulative; life events are totalled to arrive at a stress score. The greater the total amount of stress experienced, the greater the presumed likelihood of a negative outcome. The SRE and the RLCQ have been used to investigate the relationships between social stress and a variety of outcomes, including physical illness and psychological well-being.

TABLE 1-1.   Schedule of Recent Events.

Event	Weight	Event	Weight
Death of spouse	100	Change in work responsibilities	29
Divorce	73	Son or daughter leaving home	29
Marital separation	65	Trouble with in-laws	28
Jail term	63	Outstanding personal achievement	28
Death of close family member	63	Spouse begins or stops work	26
Personal injury or illness	53	Starting or finishing school	26
Marriage	50	Change in living conditions	25
Fired from work	47	Revision of personal habits	24
Marital reconciliation	45	Trouble with boss	23
Retirement	45	Change in work hours or	
Change in family members' health	44	conditions	20
		Change in residence	20
Pregnancy	40	Change in schools	20
Sex difficulties	39	Change in recreational habits	19
Addition to family	39	Change in church activities	19
Business readjustment	39	Change in social activities	18
Change in financial status	38	Mortgage or loan under $10,000	17
Death of close friend	37	Change in sleep habits	16
Change to different line of work	36	Change in number of family gatherings	15
Change in number of marital arguments	35	Change in eating habits	15
		Vacation	13
Mortgage or loan over $10,000	31	Christmas season	12
Foreclosure of mortgage or loan	30	Minor violation of the law	11

"The Social Readjustment Rating Scale," by T. H. Holmes and R. H. Rahe, *Journal of Psychosomatic Research*, 1967, *11*, 213–218. Copyright 1967 by Pergamon Press, Ltd. Reprinted by permission.

Criticisms of Traditional Social Stress Perspectives

Just as structural perspectives of social roles have been criticized for failing to consider the subjective interpretations of individuals, the traditional view of social stress has been criticized for failing to consider subjective perceptions of stress and situational factors (House, 1974; Lowenthal, Thurnher, & Chiriboga, 1975). The traditional social stress perspective assumes that a given life event has the same impact on everyone who experiences it, regardless of the individual and the circumstances. Other theorists, using a more interactionist perspective, focus on the *meaning* of events. They suggest that the impact of a particular event will vary across individuals and situations and that it's important to discover the conditions under which certain events lead to negative outcomes. The perception of stress is one critical factor. For example, retirement may be perceived as stressful by individuals who enjoy their work and have substantial investments in occupational identity, whereas it is welcomed by individuals who view their jobs as drudgery. For the first group, retirement signifies stress; however, for the second group, retirement signifies relief from stress. Consequently, we would not expect retirement to have the same impact on both groups.

The social stress perspective is compatible with the study of role changes and role transitions. Insights from social stress theory and research will continue to inform our efforts to develop a model of social adjustment in later life.

Role Transitions in Later Life

A variety of role changes and role transitions are linked to age, or to particular stages of the life cycle. In some cases, there is an inherent link between age, or life stage, and status. For example, parenthood is precluded before puberty. Statuses that are intrinsically linked to age are quite rare. Statuses and roles that are socially assigned on the basis of age or are associated with age are far more common. In our society, legal-age criteria are used to determine eligibility for certain statuses. Age criteria exist for such activities as driving a car, voting for public officials, and receiving retirement benefits. In other cases, age is not a socially defined criterion for status occupancy but is associated with the status in question. Widowhood, for example, tends to be associated with late life; however, the link between widowhood and life state is not inherent—there *are* young widows.

The information we have concerning role transitions in later life at first appears to be contradictory. The limited available research utilizing measures of social stress such as the SRE and RLCQ suggests that older adults experience fewer life events (many of which involve role transitions) than younger adults (Lowenthal et al., 1975). Such findings might lead us to the conclusion that later life is less stressful than earlier stages of the life cycle; however, several major role transitions are typically associated with later life. Widowhood, retirement, and institutionalization are three major role transitions that commonly occur in old age. Other role changes and transitions also are likely to take place during later life, including the deaths of friends or relatives, changes in residence, the departure of children from the home, and the birth of grandchildren. It is also important to note that the loss of roles is typically more common in later life than the acquisition of roles.

Although later life isn't characterized by a great number of role transitions and role changes, a few major transitions are frequently experienced during this life stage. These transitions provide a context in which social adjustment can be examined.

Review Questions

1. If a sociologist using a structural perspective observed your routines, how would he or she describe your major roles? How would someone using an interactionist perspective describe your major roles?
2. Most people marry during adulthood. What are the major socializing experiences that prepare individuals for the role of spouse? Do males and females undergo similar socializing experiences?
3. Consider the status and role of grandparent. In what ways does the grandparent role require role-taking? In what ways does the grandparent role involve role-making?
4. Visit a nursing home or a rest home and observe the activities and behavior of the residents. What are the major role duties and privileges of those residents?
5. How do the role expectations associated with being a son or daughter change as individuals progress through the life cycle?

2

Identity
and
Social
Adjustment

Unlike role behavior, the attitudes, values, and thoughts associated with social roles are not directly observable; they are subjective phenomena that must be reported to others. This chapter addresses two subjective phenomena that are related to roles and role transitions: **identity** and **adjustment.**

Identity

In order to understand the meaning of the term *identity,* it is necessary to understand a set of terms—identity, self-concept, and self-esteem—and the relationships among them. Individuals are able to think of themselves as objects—to describe their characteristics and evaluate themselves in terms of those characteristics. (For example, I could describe myself as a good scholar and a poor typist.) The notions of self-concept, self-esteem, and identity all rest on this cognitive capacity to describe and evaluate ourselves as objects.

Self-concept and *self-esteem* refer to cognitive and affective aspects of self-perception. **Self-concept** refers to the cognitive aspects of self-perception and consists of individuals' perceptions of themselves as objects. **Self-esteem** refers to the affective and evaluative aspects of self-perception and consists of judgments made about the self as an object. In practice, self-concept and self-esteem are often difficult to distinguish. For example, when I report that I am a poor typist, I appear to be both describing and evaluating my typing abilities.

Self-concept and self-esteem can be reported either in global terms or in terms of specific dimensions. *Global self-concept* refers to individuals' wholistic descriptions or perceptions of themselves. Similarly, self-esteem refers to generalized evaluations about the self as a whole. Global approaches to the definition and measurement of self-concept and self-esteem assume that individuals are able to make assessments that encompass numerous personal qualities and arrive at a general determination of the overall state of affairs —in essence, a "state of the self" message.

Self-concept and self-esteem also can be approached in terms of particular substantive dimensions. Since people are able to examine themselves in terms of any attribute or characteristic presented to them, the number of potential dimensions of self-concept and self-esteem are virtually infinite. Individuals can reflect on their performance of particular roles or evaluate themselves in terms of particular attributes. Not every role or attribute is likely to be personally significant; nonetheless, people can describe and evaluate themselves in such terms.

Presumably, global self-assessments and dimension-specific self-assessments are closely related. If you are aware of an individual's self-perception and self-evaluation with regard to all relevant dimensions, you should be able to predict his or her global self-concept and self-esteem. An assumption that underlies this line of reasoning is that an individual's global self-assessment approximates the average of his or her dimension-specific self-assessments; however, there are two caveats to be entered with regard to this assumption. First, it may be very difficult to become aware of *all* the relevant dimensions. Second, the assumption that all dimensions are equally important is questionable. Since self-conception and self-evaluation are subjective, only the individual is able to know with certainty which attributes and characteristics are relevant to his or her global self-perception and self-assessment, and only the individual knows the relative importance of those attributes and characteristics.

As it is used here, the concept of identity can help to clarify this problem. **Identity** refers to the configuration of self-perceptions and self-evaluations that are important and meaningful to the individual. Self-concept thus refers to the cognitive process of self-perception and the description of oneself as an object. Self-esteem refers to the evaluative assessment of oneself as an object. Identity refers to those self-perceptions and self-assessments that are significant to the individual. It includes both cognitive and affective components—there are identity-perceptions and identity-assessments. In other words, when I report that I am a poor typist, I make a dimension-specific self-perception and self-evaluation; however, in order to know how this relates to my sense of identity, I must also determine how important the ability to type is to me.

Identity has both content (the specific dimensions of life experience that are important to the individual) and organization (the relationships among valued dimensions of life experience). Two important components of the organization of identity are a hierarchy of importance and a hierarchy of pervasiveness. The hierarchy of importance refers to the priorities an individual places on particular dimensions of life experience. For example, my role as a teacher and my role as a Girl Scout leader may both be relevant, but I can probably specify which of those roles is more important to my identity. Identity dimensions also differ in terms of scope, or pervasiveness. Some identity dimensions are so broad that they overlay virtually all behavior and social interactions (for example, my identity as a woman), whereas others are more narrow in scope (such as my identity as a Phi Beta Kappa). Both the content and the organization of identity differ from one particular individual to another.

Epstein (1973) focuses on the organization of identity and suggests that identity is actually a theory about oneself. "It is a theory that the individual has unwittingly constructed about himself as an experiencing, functioning individual; and it is part of a broader theory which he holds with respect to his entire range of significant experience" (p. 407). Identity, according to Epstein, operates to maximize pleasure, to facilitate a sense of self-worth, and to organize life experiences in order to make them comprehensible. Epstein's description of identity as a theory permits him to describe the organization of identity in terms of the same _tandards used to describe other theories. "All theories can be evaluated by the degree to which they are extensive, parsimonious, empirically valid, internally consistent, testable, and useful. Accordingly, it should be of interest to examine self-theories of individuals with respect to each of these attributes" (p. 408). Epstein's work represents a creative and important contribution to our understanding of the organization of identity and its implications for personal well-being.

The distinctions among self-concept, self-esteem, and identity become crucial when we interpret and compare individuals' responses to self-related measuring instruments. There are three primary approaches to the measurement of self-related constructs. One common approach is to ask individuals to describe or evaluate themselves on a number of dimensions in terms of self-concept or self-esteem. When this approach is used, the subjects provide no information concerning the relevance of those dimensions to their personal identities. For example, we might ask a group of persons to relate their self-perceptions and self-assessments as employees—to specify whether they are productive, loyal, and so on. The results of such a survey would help us to compare occupational self-concept and self-esteem among employees; however, on the basis of that information, we wouldn't be able to determine how important occupation is to the employees. Undoubtedly, individuals differ in this regard. For some individuals, occupation is the cornerstone of identity; for others, it is irrelevant. Therefore, although this first approach would yield information about individuals in terms of occupational self-concept and self-esteem, it wouldn't provide information about identity.

A second approach is to ask individuals to formulate global descriptions and assessments of themselves according to a specific set of categories. For example, individuals might be asked to respond to the statement "Overall, I think I am a person of worth" by choosing *strongly agree, agree, disagree, or strongly disagree*. In the process of choosing a response, individuals undoubtedly consider those dimensions of life experience that are most relevant to their personal identity. The responses, then, provide information that is identity-relevant—information that can be compared across individuals, since a standardized set of response categories is used. Since the content of identity differs across individuals, however, comparisons of assessments are based on different and unknown referents.

A third approach requires individuals to describe and evaluate themselves in an open-ended manner. One commonly used open-ended question is "Who Am I?" (Kuhn & McPartland, 1954). In this case, individuals list the responses they believe best answer that question. Responses to such open-ended questions are presumably identity-relevant, since the individual chooses the responses. By using this type of measurement, it's possible to discover those dimensions of life experience that are important to each individual's identity. But, because there is no standardized set of responses in this method, it's very difficult to compare one individual's responses with another's.

Each of these three approaches can yield valuable information about an individual's subjective life; however, it's important to remember that each approach generates a particular kind of self-related information.

Identity Formation

Identity is typically viewed as a product of socialization that arises from social interaction and the evaluations of significant others. Socialization teaches the skills and attitudes needed for adequate role performance and generates a sense of self-in-role. When socialization is successful, individuals learn to act in accordance with behavioral expectations and to adopt those role expectations as part of their identity. From this perspective, socialization has been described as the process of teaching people to want to do what society wants them to do. In this respect, identity leads to social control and conformity: as individuals adopt given identities, they learn to value commendable role performance and to monitor their behavior in accordance with internalized expectations. External rewards and punishments become less crucial as individuals monitor their own behavior.

Socialization doesn't always result in identity formation or behavioral conformity. At times, individuals conform to behavioral standards without internalizing those standards. For example, "fair weather friends" conform to the standards of friendship until a period of crisis or stress arises. As Goffman (1959) and others have pointed out, behavior itself tells the observer little about identity; therefore, it certainly isn't safe to assume identity investments on the basis of conformity. Only the individual has direct access to his or her identity. As long as an individual conforms to behavioral expectations, it is impossible for an observer to determine whether or not such behavior reflects identity investments.

Similarly, inadequate role performance doesn't necessarily imply that a given role is irrelevant to a person's identity. A number of factors could prevent conformity, even when one's identity is invested in adequate role performance. (Some situations that result in inadequate role performance were discussed in Chapter 1.) Persons who have invested their identity in particular roles undoubtedly find inadequate role performance more distressing than persons who haven't made such an investment. In general, then, behavior is most conforming, stable, and predictable when individuals have identity investments in particular roles or activities.

Since identity is viewed as a product of socialization, roles have traditionally been linked to the notion of identity. Individuals enact roles and develop role-identities. Some authors contend that identity is necessarily linked to roles (see Burke and Tully, 1977). Other theorists view roles as a category of experience within which identity investments can develop. According to this broader perspective, identity is a product of an individual's entire social history, including general interaction experiences as well as explicit socialization efforts.

Identity Maintenance

Much human behavior and social interaction is *identity directed*— motivated by a desire to maintain and enhance identity. Of course, not all behavior is identity directed. Behavior can be task oriented or determined by simple routine. In contrast to these kinds of behavior, identity-directed behavior reflects personal values and commitments. A major mechanism of identity maintenance consists of acting and interacting in ways that are compatible with personal commitments.

Identity maintenance is often dependent on the opinions and reactions of others. For example, it's difficult for a man to believe that he is a specimen of physical strength when his audience indicates that the term *weakling* describes him perfectly. Individuals are often able to select an audience that facilitates identity maintenance. Being a "big fish in a small pond" can enhance an established identity. Moreover, an individual can structure the immediate environment so that it is conducive to identity maintenance. Consider, for example, an older person who finds it difficult to climb stairs but doesn't wish to appear disabled or infirm. If his or her public life can be restricted to places without stairs, a sense and image of physical competence can be fostered. Individuals can select social and physical environments that minimize possibilities of identity threat.

Rosenberg (1968) has pointed out that identity maintenance also is facilitated by psychological selectivity. Individuals often are able to choose situations in which their strong points and natural talents are perceived as *identity relevant*, whereas their weak points are defined as *identity irrelevant*. Psychological selectivity also can influence the interpretation of evidence concerning identity. To some degree, we are able to determine what constitutes relevant evidence as well as the appropriate interpretation of that evidence. Psychological selectivity can thus block evidence that suggests performance is not compatible with identity investments. Finally, psychological selectivity can determine the aspired level of performance. If a discrepancy between aspirations and achievements poses an identity problem, a lowering of aspirations can resolve the problem just as well as an elevation of achievement.

Behavioral and psychological selectivity are most likely to be employed in situations that are relatively unstructured and in which the range of acceptable behavior is wide. These techniques help individuals to maintain a positive sense of identity, and they demonstrate the importance of the individual in the process of identity formation and maintenance. Identity-directed behavior, then, cannot be understood solely in terms of conformity to behavioral expectations or the desire for social approval.

The Interface between Roles and Identity

Identity is often directly related to the statuses we occupy and the roles we perform. Although identity can be related to life experiences other than social roles, socialization to particular roles can result in identity formation as well as the adoption of the skills and attitudes relevant to adequate role performance. Once formulated, identity influences the selection of subsequent roles and statuses and becomes a major motivational force in behavior.

Identity also helps to clarify the conditions under which role changes or transitions are perceived and experienced as stressful. Loss of or changes in roles that are personally significant are more stressful than loss of or changes in roles that don't involve substantial identity investment. Moreover, since identity differs from one individual to another, consideration of identity can help to determine why a given role change or transition (such as retirement) may be perceived as stressful by one individual but not by another. This relates directly to the sense of loss that is associated with some role shifts and transitions (see Chapter 1).

Social adjustment is characterized by two conditions: first, the individual meets the demands of the environment; and second, the individual perceives and experiences a sense of general well-being in relation to the environment. Maladjustment can occur when the individual cannot meet the level of environmental demands or can do so only at the cost of personal well-being. Adjustment has both objective and subjective components. The degree to which the individual meets environmental demands is an objective phenomenon, whereas perceptions of well-being are subjective.

Like identity, adjustment is a major motivational factor in human behavior and social interaction. A great deal of behavior is determined by efforts to meet the demands of the environment or to maintain a sense of personal well-being. As defined here, then, adjustment is a very broad concept that encompasses almost all human behavior. This conceptual breadth has both strengths and weaknesses. Its strength lies in the obvious significance of the concept for understanding human behavior. Difficulties arise in defining and measuring adjustment for purposes of research and understanding particular situations.

It's extremely difficult to define and measure the degree to which an individual meets the demands of his or her environment; it is a task that requires some criteria for rating the adequacy of behavior. The problem is complicated by the fact that behavior that is appropriate in one situation may be inadequate in a different situation. For example, an individual might need to employ a complex and sophisticated set of behaviors in order to deal with crises, whereas this same set of behaviors might not be needed in meeting the demands of everyday life. Inevitably, then, an examination of specific behaviors cannot provide information about adjustment unless those behaviors are examined in the context of a particular situation. The adequacy of role performance can be considered one measure of the degree to which environmental demands are being met.

The second component of adjustment—a sense of personal well-being —also is a broad concept that presents difficulty in terms of definition and measurement. One explanation for this difficulty is the fact that a sense of well-being is largely determined by personal preference and taste. For example, a job that involves working with people may be important to my sense of well-being, but irrelevant to someone else's. In many ways, however, this issue is a false argument. A growing body of literature suggests that, in our society, people *do* use very similar criteria in their assessments of the quality of life (Andrews & Withey, 1976; Campbell, Converse, & Rodgers, 1976). Respondents in several large national surveys have identified certain areas of life experience, including work, family, leisure activities, and a sense of community, as important factors in their assessments of personal well-being.

Moreover, although individuals differ to some degree in terms of the conditions they consider relevant to a sense of well-being, reports of their perceptions of personal well-being can be collected in a standardized manner and compared.

In previous studies, a variety of concepts have been used to measure perceptions of well-being. The most frequently used approach requires individuals to rate their current level of life satisfaction—the degree to which they find life in general satisfying or dissatisfying. Individuals presumably base reports of life satisfaction on those aspects of life and the environment that are most important to them. Evidence suggests that assessments of life satisfaction are based on a comparison of the actual conditions of life to an aspired or imagined ideal set of life conditions (see Campbell et al., 1976). A large body of literature indicates that reports of life satisfaction are associated with objective indicators of environmental conditions as well as measures of subjective well-being.

The measurement of happiness is related to the measurement of personal well-being—both happiness and life satisfaction require an assessment of the experience of life in general. However, in contrast to life satisfaction, happiness reflects a transitory and affective state of euphoria or gaiety. Life satisfaction refers to an individual's concept of life in a cognitive rather than an emotional sense and, therefore, is probably a more direct, stable, and accurate approach to defining perceptions of well-being.

Life satisfaction, like self-concept and self-esteem, may be assessed globally (in reference to life in general) or in terms of specific areas of life (work, family, and so on). Two recent studies support the assumption that global assessments of life satisfaction are related to domain-specific reports of satisfaction (Andrews & Withey, 1976; Campbell et al., 1976). It is important to remember that global assessments might not be sufficiently sensitive for some purposes. For example, job advancement would be expected to be more closely related to domain-specific satisfaction with work than with global assessments of life satisfaction.

The Interface between
Identity and Adjustment

A number of parallels exist between identity and adjustment. Both are subjective phenomena that are directly available only to the individual. Both can be assessed globally or in terms of specific dimensions or domains. Life satisfaction is associated with identity in that individuals base their assessments of satisfaction on those domains of life that are important to their identity and their aspirations.

Both identity and adjustment involve dynamic processes of change and negotiation as well as static states of being. When used in a static sense, *identity* and *adjustment* refer to an individual's current sense of identity or level of adjustment. However, identity and adjustment are subject to change as individuals experience and interpret new situations. Identity is not only a theory about the self; it is also a process of organizing and interpreting self-related perceptions and evaluations. Likewise, adjustment is not only a state of congruence between the individual and the environment; it is also a process of striving for congruence.

Identity assessments are undoubtedly related to perceptions of well-being. It would be difficult for most of us to be satisfied with our lives if we were dissatisfied with ourselves or if our identities were under attack. However, identity and perceptions of well-being are conceptually distinct. A sense of personal well-being refers to the conditions of life, whereas a sense of self-worth refers specifically to the conditions of the self.

The Interface between Roles and Adjustment

The links between social roles and adjustment have not been well defined. As I noted previously, role demands are one kind of environmental demand; therefore, adequacy of role performance is one measure of the objective component of adjustment.

Role changes and role transitions represent a second area of interface between roles and adjustment. Since role changes and transitions are a kind of environmental demand, they may trigger adjustment processes. Even role changes and transitions that don't pose a threat to identity can pose adaptive challenges. For example, loss of an unpleasant job (which doesn't threaten identity) might require decisions on issues such as how to distribute increased amounts of leisure time or how to acquire a new source of livelihood.

Identity and Adjustment in Later Life

Very little evidence is available concerning the effects of aging on identity and adjustment. Most available studies compare persons of different ages rather than follow the same individuals over time in order to observe change. As a result, statements about identity and adjustment in later life must be stated cautiously.

Traditionally, investigators have expected the social and physical losses commonly associated with aging to result in negative self-evaluations and losses of identity; however, available evidence suggests that self-concept and self-esteem remain remarkably stable over time. Although some individuals do experience dramatic changes in self-perception and self-evaluation, the more common pattern is continuity over time. Evidence concerning identity in later life is even more scarce than the evidence concerning self-concept and self-esteem. Some research suggests that investments in certain roles change as individuals pass through the life cycle, but more common findings suggest that persons continue to value the same identity-relevant activities throughout adulthood. Undoubtedly, the identity-maintaining strategies described earlier —identity-directed behavior and psychological selectivity—help to maintain stability in identity, self-concept, and self-esteem.

Evidence relevant to adjustment throughout the life cycle is somewhat more plentiful, but, again, much of the data is derived from cross-sectional studies and must be interpreted with caution. The ability to meet environmental demands—the objective component of adjustment—appears to decrease somewhat with age. Decreases in physical energy, decrements in health, and other factors commonly associated with aging affect the individual's ability to respond to environmental demands. Therefore, functional capacity, as it is variously defined in diverse areas, typically decreases as individuals grow older.

Fortunately, this doesn't mean that older people are typically unable to meet the demands of their environments. The fact is that most of us, regardless of age, are able to function effectively without pushing our capacities to their limits. We are able to meet the routine challenges of the environment without utilizing our full battery of personal resources. (Chapter 3 focuses on personal resources. At this point, it is sufficient to note that resources usually exceed demands.)

The fact that most older people are able to meet the demands of their environments is supported by reports of life satisfaction—one indicator of the subjective component of adjustment—in later life. In surveys of adults in the U. S., the vast majority of older persons report high levels of life satisfaction. In fact, older adults frequently report higher levels of life satisfaction than young and middle-aged persons.

The distinction between life satisfaction and happiness is relevant to the assessment of perceived well-being. Campbell et al. (1976) examined differences in life satisfaction and happiness among adults of all ages, ranging from early adulthood to old age. The intriguing results of this survey, presented in Figure 2-1, indicate that younger and older adults report very different levels of well-being. Young adults (age 18–24 and 25–34) report higher levels of happiness than the sample as a whole—especially higher than the older adults. However, older respondents (age 65–74 and 75 and older) report higher levels of life satisfaction than the sample as a whole—especially higher than young adults. These results suggest that old age is a period of relatively low levels of happiness and high levels of life satisfaction. In contrast, young adulthood is characterized by relatively high levels of happiness and low levels of life satisfaction. These data suggest that euphoria is the prerogative

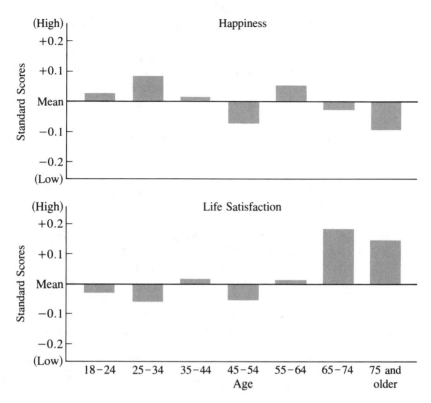

FIGURE 2-1   Average levels of happiness and life satisfaction, by age (expressed as deviations from average of whole sample). (Figure 2.4 in The Quality of American Life: Perceptions, Evaluations and Satisfactions, *by Campbell et al., © 1976 by Russell Sage Foundation, New York. Reprinted by permission of Basic Books, Inc., Publishers.)*

of youth, whereas contentment is the reward of old age. It's interesting to note that both life satisfaction and happiness are quite low during middle age. Apparently, middle-aged individuals no longer have the fleeting pleasures of youth and haven't yet attained the tranquility of later life.

Although Figure 2-1 suggests significant differences in happiness and life satisfaction across the life cycle, these data should be interpreted with caution. The data reported in Figure 2-1 weren't based on changes in the same individuals over time; therefore, differences may be due to factors other than age. In any case, the data clearly demonstrate that happiness and life satisfaction are distinct phenomena.

This review of identity and adjustment across the life cycle reaffirms their importance as both process and state. When identity and adjustment are measured at one point in time, evidence of identity states and levels of adjustment is gathered. Such reports inevitably miss the processive elements of identity and adjustment change. Existing data from short-term longitudinal studies suggest that both identity and adjustment are responsive to changes in life conditions. When challenges are experienced, personal efforts become directed toward achieving and maintaining a positive sense of identity and a compatible relationship with the physical and social environment. It is this characteristic of identity and adjustment—the tendency toward stable states, combined with sensitivity and responsiveness to external elements—that makes these concepts important elements in a theory of social adjustment in later life.

Review Questions

1. *Social scientists often describe adolescence as a life stage characterized by a "search for identity." Similarly, recent speculation about a "midlife crisis" focuses on issues of identity. Given the definition of identity used in this chapter, how might issues of identity be linked to these life stages?*
2. *Mr. P likes to think of himself as a first-rate carpenter. In actuality, his work would not pass local building codes. What kinds of mechanisms might Mr. P be using to convince himself that his building skills are deserving of praise?*
3. *What is the difference between happiness and life satisfaction? Which one of the two is a better indicator of the subjective component of adjustment? Why?*
4. *Persons who are incarcerated, committed to mental hospitals, or inducted into the armed forces often complain that they have been stripped of their identity. What does this mean?*
5. *Epstein suggests that each of us has a theory about who we are and what we are like. Describe your theory of yourself.*

3

Resources, Coping Skills, and Social Status Factors

As we begin to assemble the elements of a model of social adjustment to role transitions in later life, it's important that we note the complexities involved. Some of these complexities are due to the wide variety of role transitions experienced in late adulthood; others reflect the dynamic processes of identity change and maintenance and the diverse configurations of person/environment fit. The personal characteristics of individuals and the contexts within which role transitions occur also must be taken into account. A given role transition (widowhood, for example) is experienced by persons of widely varying backgrounds and personal qualities in disparate situational contexts. It should not be surprising, then, that widowhood has varied effects on adjustment and identity. This chapter focuses on three factors that affect an individual's adjustment to role transitions: personal resources, coping skills, and social-status factors.

Personal Resources

Personal resources are the broad range of reserves and aids individuals can draw on in times of need. Since they are mobilized in order to alleviate difficulties, resources are closely related to perceptions of stress. When individuals have sufficient appropriate resources, they aren't likely to view a potentially stressful situation as problematic. In cases of more serious threat, resources can either lessen the impact of a stressful situation or lead to a swifter and smoother adjustment to that situation. Situations for which individuals lack resources are most likely to be perceived and defined as stressful.

Resources can take a variety of forms, depending on the particular source of stress and the situation in which the stress occurs. A resource might prove effective in one situation but ineffective in another; however, a number of resources are effective in a variety of situations. Four of these—financial resources, health, social support, and education—are discussed in the following paragraphs.

Financial Resources. Financial assets serve as a resource in a wide range of potentially stressful situations. Money can be used to purchase a variety of specific resources that are directly relevant to particular situations. For example, money cannot repair a car; however, with adequate financial assets, the owner of a car can purchase the necessary repairs, procure an alternative means of transportation during repairs, or even buy another car. For the person who lacks adequate financial resources, the breakdown of a car can be a stressful experience. For the person who has adequate financial resources, the need for repairs is a mere inconvenience.

Health. Conventional wisdom suggests that health is frequently taken for granted. Health alone certainly cannot solve most of the problems encountered in everyday life. Rather, health seems to be conspicuous by its absence. Usually, individuals aren't aware of the part good health plays in affecting the impact of potentially stressful situations until they experience illness or disability. The role of physical well-being as a resource is especially important in later life, because health tends to become increasingly problematic during that life stage.

Social Support. In order to understand the ways in which social support operates as a resource, it's necessary to distinguish **social networks** from **social support systems.** Social networks are patterns of social involvement—the configuration of people with whom an individual maintains regular contact. Social support systems are made up of individuals who provide help during times of need or stress. All the members of an individual's social network aren't necessarily potential sources of support. At times, people might be unwilling or unable to provide needed help.

Social support systems involve a rather special sense of commitment to an individual. Two kinds of commitment that generate social support are bonds of affection and ties of obligation. Bonds of affection are typically the basis of commitment in informal social support systems, such as groups of friends and neighbors. Ties of obligation are more likely to be the basis of commitment among formal sources of support, such as doctors, social workers, and other providers of services. In reality, of course, bonds of affection and ties of obligation frequently coexist; for example, reciprocal obligations often operate among friends. Family relationships also are typically characterized by both obligation and affection.

Social support systems can provide a variety of resources, ranging from specific services to a general sense of emotional sustenance. The personal qualities of the members of a support system determine, in large degree, the quality of that system as a resource. If the persons to whom one can turn for help are "resource poor," it's unlikely that they will be willing or able to provide adequate support. If, on the other hand, the members of a social support system are "resource rich," they will be better able to provide help in solving problems.

Education. Education can help to alleviate stress in two ways. First, education is directed toward teaching skills that can be used to confront stressful situations. Second, education appears to foster a cognitive complexity that facilitates realistic stress perception and problem-solving skills (Lazarus, 1966).

The value of resources is commonly understood. Likewise, the fact that money, good health, and close personal relationships act as effective buffers in many difficult situations is widely acknowledged. Accordingly, the desire to accumulate resources and thus achieve a sense of security can be an important motivational factor in human behavior and social interaction. Most of us attempt to stockpile at least a moderate reserve of resources that we can draw upon in time of need.

The loss of resources is often a source of social stress. Good health is a resource; poor health indicates a lack of resources and can be a stressful situation in and of itself. The loss of a job can be a stressful role loss as well as a threat to an individual's economic security.

Personal Resources
in Later Life

Levels of personal resources vary widely among younger and older persons in our society; nonetheless, as a group, older persons tend to have lower levels of resources than younger adults. Some of these lower levels appear to be associated with the aging process (for example, declines in health), whereas others reflect the consequences of social patterns and practices (such as reductions in income subsequent to retirement) and group characteristics (such as differences between age groups that reflect customs or historical circumstances) of the current younger and older populations (differences in average levels of educational attainment, for example).

TABLE 3-1.   Median Income of United States Families, by Age: 1967, 1972, and 1977.

Age	1967	1972	1977
14–24	$5,844	$ 7,447	$10,376
25–34	8,095	11,161	15,828
35–44	9,239	13,119	18,862
45–54	9,676	14,056	20,832
55–65	8,042	11,675	17,221
65 and older	3,728	5,968	9,110
Total (all ages)	$7,974	$14,614	$16,009

(From *Consumer Income Reports, Current Population Surveys,* Series P-60, No. 59, April 1968; No. 90, December 1973; No. 116, July 1978. U. S. Bureau of the Census. Washington, D. C.: U. S. Government Printing Office.)

In terms of financial resources, older individuals are at a disadvantage relative to both other age groups in the population and to their own cohort at previous life stages. As Table 3-1 indicates, although family income has increased steadily over the past 15 years for persons of all ages, the substantial gap between median income levels of older and younger persons has remained essentially the same. In other words, although there have been absolute increases in the levels of income available to older persons, their position relative to other age groups remains low. Retirement, of course, has a substantial impact on the financial situation of older persons, usually resulting in a 50% reduction in income (Streib, 1976; Hendricks & Hendricks, 1977).

Measures of net worth, which include such factors as property, savings, and investments, indicate that both younger (25–44) and older (65 and older) persons tend to have lower levels of net worth than do middle-aged persons (Institute of Interdisciplinary Studies, 1974). Apparently, young adulthood is characterized by resource accumulation, whereas later life is a period of financial dissipation, although differences in net worth also reflect cohort differences.

Decline in physical well-being is common during later life. As Table 3-2 shows, chronic diseases, which are unlikely to be cured and which typically impair functional ability, are particularly common occurrences at advanced ages. Most older persons suffer from at least one chronic illness, and many others are victims of multiple chronic conditions (U. S. Department of HEW, 1972). Along with declines in functional status, decreases in physical vigor and general energy levels beset most older individuals. Moreover, most older individuals experience a decrease in the effectiveness of their sensory processes (Hendricks & Hendricks, 1977). In general, then, although the majority of older persons are functionally capable of independent living, they are likely to experience some physical deterioration.

TABLE 3-2. Percent of Population with Limitations of Activity due to Chronic Conditions, by Age.

Age	No Activity Limitation	Some Limitation In Activity	Limitation In Major Activity
16 and younger	96.6	3.4	1.8
17–44	91.9	8.1	5.2
45–64	76.9	23.1	18.6
65 and older	57.0	43.0	37.3
Total (all ages)	86.5	13.5	10.4

(Adapted from *Current Estimates from the Health Interview Survey: United States, 1977*, Series 10, No. 126, p. 24. National Center for Health Statistics, Health Resources Administration. Washington, D. C.: U. S. Government Printing Office, 1978.)

Most older persons maintain active involvement in social networks, live with their spouse, enjoy frequent and satisfying contact with their children, and participate in informal friendship and voluntary organization networks (Lowenthal & Robinson, 1976). Although a social network isn't necessarily a social support system, most older persons maintain meaningful social ties that facilitate the development of social support systems. On the other hand, however, evidence suggests that a minority of older persons are without sources of social support. In some cases, this appears to reflect long-term patterns of social isolation; however, in other cases, the absence of social support is apparently due to age-related losses of significant others (Lowenthal & Robinson, 1976).

Sussman (1976) suggests that social support systems, especially the family, play a special role in assisting older people to obtain appropriate social services. In modern societies, many publicly funded services are available to either the older population as a whole or to certain needy subgroups of the older population. In order to use such services, older individuals need to be aware of the programs and be able to manipulate bureaucratic procedures. Sussman suggests that, in modern societies, family members play a decreasing role in providing direct services to older people, but they play an increasingly important role in mediating between older persons and service bureaucracies. Sussman's propositions are supported by a study of family relationships and the use of services among American Indians (Murdock & Schwartz, 1978). Data collected in that study show that the actual need for social services was especially great among older persons who lived alone. In spite of this fact, the perceived need for services, awareness of available service programs, and actual use of services was highest among older persons who lived with their family members. Social support systems provide resources and services and mobilize potential resources in the community.

Individuals differ in the ways in which they react to stressful or potentially stressful situations. Some people "fall apart" and are unable to cope with the slightest difficulty, whereas others appear to handle even the most difficult situations with grace and competence. In spite of the obvious significance of the personal styles individuals use to confront stressful situations, behavioral scientists have only begun to describe and understand coping, and they are still largely unable to assess the effectiveness of specific coping strategies.

One factor that contributes to ambiguity in this area is the way in which **coping** has been defined. Some authors distinguish between intrapsychic (or emotional) and behavioral responses to stressful situations and view only the latter as coping (see French, Rodgers, & Cobb, 1974; Mechanic, 1970). Similarly, some authors have defined coping as an effort to alter a stressful situation. These authors view attempts to alleviate anxiety and secure comfort as defenses or stress management rather than coping. One of the problems associated with this type of definition is that, in practice, the distinction is often difficult to make. For example, when an individual alters a stressful situation, he or she also alters the perception of stress. In order to examine the entire range of strategies individuals use in responding to stress, a more inclusive definition will be used here. Following the lead of McGrath (1970a [p. 33]), we will define **coping** as the covert and overt behaviors individuals use to prevent, alleviate, or respond to stressful situations. This definition encompasses behaviors directed toward altering the perception of stress and the emotional distress associated with life problems as well as efforts to alleviate stressful situations. Since coping skills are used to respond to stress, they can be viewed as valuable personal resources. (The issue of coping is so directly relevant to stress and adjustment, however, that it will be discussed separately.)

Temporal Issues

Coping can occur before, during, or after a stressful situation (McGrath, 1970b). *Preventive coping* is used to deter a potentially stressful situation. When a stressful situation can't be prevented, *anticipatory coping* can sometimes alleviate some impact. Anticipatory coping refers to efforts directed toward "easing the blow," or preparing in advance. Finally, coping responses can (and usually do) occur following a stressful situation.

Coping itself is a process. Although we lack sufficient data to fully describe the coping process, several authors have proposed general models that outline the steps involved in coping. For example, Tyler (1978) suggests a three-stage coping process. First, during the "search and organize" stage, an individual seeks out and evaluates behavioral alternatives. Then, during the "implementation" stage, he or she puts new behaviors into operation. Finally, during the "culminate, conclude, and redefine" stage, the individual performs affective and cognitive tasks in order to accept the stressful situation and the way in which it has been handled. This final stage permits individuals to incorporate experiences into their identities. Janis (1974) describes a similar five-stage model of the coping process: appraise the challenge (perceive the stress), appraise the range of alternatives, reach a tentative behavioral plan, act on the behavioral plan, and adhere to the behavioral plan. These models emphasize the importance of an active, organized approach to coping. In addition, both authors indicate that omission of a stage is likely to decrease the effectiveness of the coping behavior.

Identifying Specific Coping Strategies

Some authors have attempted to classify and describe specific coping strategies. Frequently, a distinction is made between behavioral strategies and cognitive/emotional strategies (see Lazarus, 1966; Mechanic, 1974). Behavioral coping strategies include a wide variety of actions directed toward either changing stressful situations or alleviating distress. Cognitive/emotional strategies refer to the ways in which individuals alter their subjective perceptions of stressful situations. *Defense* and *denial* are used to refer to these cognitive/emotional reappraisals. Much more effort is needed to identify and describe specific coping strategies. The following research efforts by Steiner and Pearlin and Schooler provide illustrations of the directions such work could profitably take.

In a series of experiments, Steiner (Steiner, 1966; Steiner, 1970; Steiner & Johnson, 1964) identified four coping strategies individuals use when their views are contradicted by valued peers. In such cases, individuals can (1) change their views to conform to those of their peers, (2) reject their peers, viewing them as less competent than expected, (3) devalue the issue in question, or (4) deny the amount or extent of disagreement. These four strategies appear repeatedly in the series of experiments. Although different individuals use different strategies, most subjects in these experiments exhibited a clear preference for a particular strategy.

In discussing the limits of his studies, Steiner acknowledges that the four strategies he identified may or may not apply to experiences other than interpersonal disagreements and that experimental situations aren't as significant as actual disagreements in more natural settings. Nonetheless, these studies provide a clear example of the types of specific coping strategies that can and should be identified.

More recently, Pearlin and Schooler (1978) examined the coping strategies individuals use when they face problems in four specific areas: marriage, parenthood, household economics, and occupational goals and activities. Their analysis revealed three broad categories of coping responses: (1)

responses that modify situations, (2) responses that are used to reappraise the meaning of problems, and (3) responses that help individuals to manage tension. In addition, the authors noted that problems in specific areas were usually associated with specific coping responses. For example, in the area of household economics, the most effective strategies involved reappraisal of values and goals (such as devaluing the importance of money or substituting rewards). On the other hand, in the areas of marriage and parenthood, these same strategies were used less frequently and proved to be less effective. Direct-action strategies proved more valuable. These results support Steiner's theory that coping strategies differ across areas of life experience.

Personality and Attitudinal Factors

Coping includes personality, or attitudinal, components as well as the use of specific strategies. In contrast to behavioral alternatives and strategies, which probably differ according to the nature of the stress and the area of life experience involved, the personality or attitudinal component consists of more general and stable personal predispositions. Researchers have identified three general classes of predispositions: personality traits, attitudes, and beliefs.

Personality Traits. Four personality traits have been identified as important elements of coping styles: chronic anxiety (Hamburg, Coelho, & Adams, 1974; Lazarus, 1966), openness to new experience (Hamburg et al., 1974; Jahoda, 1958), impulse control (Lazarus, 1966), and a tendency to deny the experience of threat (Lazarus, 1966; White, 1974). High levels of chronic anxiety are detrimental to effective coping for a number of reasons. Anxiety is likely to sensitize an individual to the perception of stress, interfere with the appraisal of relevant behavioral alternatives, and hinder an individual's ability to implement behavioral goals. Openness to experience, which reflects an underlying acceptance of change and a flexible stance toward the environment, facilitates coping. Poor impulse control is viewed as detrimental to effective coping, because it usually precludes well-planned action that is based on adequate information about the range of behavioral alternatives. Similarly, denial is not viewed as an effective long-term coping response. The prevailing view suggests that the realities of the stressful situation will eventually resurface and that denial will have prohibited the gathering of adequate information on which to base a constructive behavioral plan.

Somewhat surprisingly, high levels of emotional sensitivity and an introspective approach to life are irrelevant to successful coping (Grinker, 1962; Mechanic, 1974). Therefore, in spite of the fact that threat to identity is often one facet of social stress, self-reflection and self-actualizing motives do not appear to be related to effective problem solving.

Attitudes. Several attitudes are relevant to coping. The most important of these is a sense of self-efficacy—a basic belief in one's ability to initiate and control personal experiences (see Jahoda, 1958; Lazarus, 1966). A number of empirical studies indicate that a sense of internal control—a perception of oneself as an active agent, in control of one's life course—is an important component of effective coping (Ezekiel, 1968; Smith, 1966; Tyler, 1978).

Beliefs. Beliefs regarding the nature of the world (the external environment) are relevant to effective coping. A sense of basic trust in the world—a perception of the world as an orderly, predictable, and responsive environment—is conducive to effective coping (Lazarus, 1966; Rotter, 1967; Tyler, 1978). Conversely, feelings of anomie or distrust hinder an active, organized coping stance.

In general, then, personality and attitudinal factors appear to operate as predispositions to the likelihood of an active, masterful coping style. Consequently, we would expect these factors to correlate highly with the behavioral coping strategies individuals choose when confronting a stressful situation.

The Interface between Coping and Socialization

Mechanic (1974) has pointed out that most of the coping literature draws heavily from the theoretical perspectives of clinical psychology, emphasizing the importance of individual behavior styles and intrapsychic states. Consequently, the structural and normative facets of coping have been relatively neglected. There is, in fact, an important link between coping and socialization.

As it is defined here, the term *coping* refers to behaviors individuals use to prevent, alleviate, or respond to stressful or challenging situations. Socialization prepares individuals for facing problematic situations by helping them to identify appropriate behaviors and acquire the skills they need to implement those behaviors. In other words, coping strategies reflect the attitudes and skills individuals gain through socialization, as well as their personal predispositions and behavioral preferences.

The Elements of Effective Coping

Much more research is needed to identify and describe the attitudinal/personality characteristics and behavioral strategies that are most effective in coping with stressful situations. Even the best substantiated correlates of effective coping, such as a sense of self-efficacy, merit further attention. It's possible that successful coping leads to a sense of self-efficacy (rather than the reverse, as is commonly presumed). More importantly, the effectiveness of particular coping strategies cannot be assessed without a model that permits observation of coping in the context of specific stressful situations and in relation to identified outcomes. Such models are discussed in Chapter 4.

Coping Skills in Later Life

Very little is known about coping skills in later life; however, there are no compelling reasons to believe that coping styles are strongly related to age. Throughout adulthood, individuals probably develop and refine a repertoire of workable coping strategies that are compatible with their personal dispositions and lifestyles. This viewpoint is suggested in two classic studies of later life. In a study of adjustment to retirement, Reichard, Livson, and Peterson (1962) described five basic types of personalities. The mature, rocking chair, and armored men exhibited adaptive personality styles: mature men were characterized by healthy realism, rocking chair personalities were passive-dependent individuals who quietly accepted life, and armored men had highly integrated defense mechanisms that shielded them from the perception of stress. The two less healthy personality styles were the angry men, who were typically bitter, rigid, and aggressive, and the self-haters, who were also angry, but who channeled their anger against themselves.

In another study, Neugarten and her associates (Neugarten, Crotty, & Tobin, 1964; Neugarten, Havighurst, & Tobin, 1968) developed a four-category typology of personality structure: integrated, passive dependent, armored defended, and unintegrated. As these labels suggest, Neugarten's categories were very similar to those of Reichard and her associates. The studies mentioned here suggest that the personality structures displayed by older persons reflect long-term, stable, coping styles.

A substantial amount of research has focused on specific attitudes or personality traits that may be relevant to coping. For example, studies have examined levels of internal versus external locus of control. The findings consistently indicate that older persons exhibit high levels of perceived internal control—higher levels than those of younger persons (see Reid, Haas, & Hawkins, 1977; Staats, 1974). Since a sense of self-efficacy is associated with effective coping, this pattern bodes well for the coping stance of most older people. However, a variety of laboratory studies suggest that older persons' coping styles are hindered by a tendency to be cautious in the face of risk and to become highly anxious when confronting performance situations (Botwinick, 1973). Although such studies provide tantalizing bits of information that are potentially relevant to the study of coping, concerted and integrated efforts to investigate the complex configuration of behaviors and attitudes that comprise coping are clearly needed.

Social Status Factors

This chapter has focused on personal resources and coping skills as two important types of factors that influence the impact of stressful life events on identity and adjustment. Social status factors also influence the impact of these events.

Social status variables represent an individual's most basic ties to social structures and social organizations. Location in the social structure, in turn, is related to numerous aspects of life experience, including stressful events, available resources and coping skills, the nature of one's identity, and level of adjustment. Examples of basic social status variables include sex, age, race, religion, and social class.

Although this book explicitly addresses the issues of stress, identity, and adjustment in the context of aging, it's important to remember that the process of adjustment is influenced by other social status factors. For example, some aspects of adjustment to retirement and widowhood are substantially different for women than they are for men.

It's difficult to predict the impact of social status variables on the process of adjustment. This contrasts sharply with our ability to predict the impact of personal resources and coping skills, which facilitate adjustment to stressful life events and role transitions. The influence of social status factors is more complex. Differences in social status are not consistently related to positive or negative outcomes. For example, we cannot assume that women have a uniform advantage over men during role transitions in the same way that we expect good health to facilitate successful adjustment to a variety of stressful life events. Instead, women might find some role transitions less difficult than men, while men experience less stress than women during other role transitions. In other words, the effects of social status variables on adjustment and identity tend to be situation specific. Consequently, it's important to determine the conditions under which particular social status factors have a positive or negative impact on personal well-being.

The influences of social status factors are difficult to interpret, because they represent broad aspects of experience and are related to other variables. For example, compared to younger adults, older people typically have lower levels of educational attainment and financial assets and are more likely to suffer disabling chronic diseases. If we found that older individuals generally found a particular role transition more stressful than younger persons, we wouldn't be able to determine whether the inherent properties of age or the age-related differences in personal resources accounted for the pattern. The interpretation of why or in what way social status factors influence adjustment is a difficult and complex process. In spite of the complexities involved, social status factors help us to determine the conditions under which role transitions and events have a negative impact on identity and adjustment. The influence of social status factors testifies to the significance of social structure for personal well-being.

Review Questions

1. *What is social support? Who are your major sources of social support and what kinds of services do they provide for you?*
2. *Some people feel that the best possible form of social intervention for older people is direct income transfers that guarantee each older person a prescribed income base. In what ways would such programs contribute to effective adjustment among older people? Are there areas of life in which such programs would not be beneficial?*
3. *In what ways might age, sex, and race influence adjustment to widowhood?*
4. *Consider the following situation: Ms. S. detects a small lump in her breast. Describe three alternative (and plausible) responses Ms. S. might make in this situation. Which alternative represents the most effective coping style? Why?*
5. *Many older persons do not eat a balanced and nutritious diet. What kinds of formal and informal resources might help to remedy this situation?*

4

Models of Social Adjustment in Later Life

The preceding chapters introduced the elements needed to examine adjustment to role transitions and stress. Age-related transitions and stresses pose potential adaptive problems for many older persons. The consequences of social stress can be understood by examining two components of personal well-being: social adjustment and identity. Finally, it was suggested that individual responses to stressful situations can be understood by taking personal resources, coping skills, and social status factors into account. In this chapter, we incorporate these elements into a theory, or model, of the social-adjustment process. This task consists of two parts. First, we need to examine proposed perspectives of social adjustment. This review will serve to further our understanding of social adjustment in later life and to identify issues that remain conceptually ambiguous. Second, an integrated model is proposed that incorporates the strengths of previous perspectives and resolves some of the remaining theoretical problems.

A model is an interrelated set of concepts intended to explain a limited area of human behavior. Conceptual models, which are testable, specify or propose the relationships that exist among concepts. The development of conceptual models lies at the heart of translating social science theory into research and, in turn, using research results to clarify and refine social science theory.

In the following sections, we will briefly review the work of Lieberman and Tobin (adaptation of life crises), Kuypers and Bengtson (labeling and social breakdown in later life), Rosow (socialization to old age), and Lowenthal, Thurnher, and Chiriboga (intentionality across the life cycle).

Social Adjustment in Later Life: A Brief Review of Previous Works

Adaptation to Life Crises: Lieberman and Tobin

Lieberman and Tobin focused their research on an effort to explain patterns of adaptations to life crises (Lieberman, 1975; Tobin & Lieberman, 1976). More specifically, they examined adaptation to changes in living arrangements among older people, especially those who were impaired. Lieberman and Tobin suggest that change in residence is potentially stressful because of the subjective experience of stress (a sense of loss) and the more objective consequences of change (the disruption of customary behavior patterns).

Figure 4-1 schematically presents the model of adaptation to life crises suggested by Lieberman and Tobin. This model both emerged from and guided their research efforts. In spite of differences in terminology, it includes all the basic concepts discussed in Chapters 1 through 3. The model is a dynamic one that suggests the importance of measuring different concepts at different stages of the adaptation process.

The model begins with an assessment of personal resources in the areas of cognitive abilities, energy levels, and biological characteristics. The assessment of current functioning is actually a baseline (or prestressor) measure of adaptation. This measure of functioning is needed in order to directly relate the effects of stress to subsequent changes in adaptation or functioning. Social support, which we have viewed as a personal resource, is included in the model as a distinct category.

Measurement of stress (in Lieberman and Tobin's work, change in residence) occurs after the baseline measure of adaptation has been obtained. Two other elements of the model, "amount and intensity of loss" and "degree of life-space change," are also apparently characteristics of the stressor, although they are conceivably indicators of the perception of stress. The measurement of "threat" refers to an individual's perceptions of the stressor.

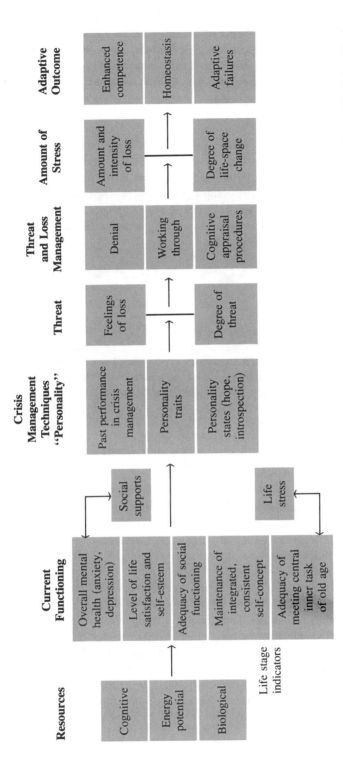

FIGURE 4-1 Lieberman and Tobin's model of adaptation to life crises. (From "Adaptive Processes in Late Life," by M. A. Lieberman. In N. Datan and L. H. Ginsberg [Eds.], Life-Span Developmental Psychology: Normative Life Crises. Copyright 1975 by Academic Press, Inc. Reprinted by permission of the author and publisher.)

Several components of the model proposed by Lieberman and Tobin are compatible with our conceptualization of coping skills presented in Chapter 3. "Crisis management techniques" and "personality" refer to relatively stable attitudinal predispositions that are relevant to the adjustment process. The category of "threat and loss management" refers to the more specific behavioral coping strategies individuals use.

The outcome level of adjustment, "adaptive outcome," is measured in the same multidimensional manner used to establish the baseline measure of functioning, in which physical, social (including identity-relevant measures of self-esteem and self-concept), and psychological indicators are examined. Since adjustment is viewed as a comparison of functioning before and after an identified crisis, three outcomes are possible: (1) enhanced competence, in which functioning is improved after a crisis; (2) homeostasis, in which functioning is at the same level before and after a crisis; or (3) adaptive failure, in which functioning is impaired as a result of a crisis.

Using this basic model, Lieberman and Tobin examined adaptation to residential relocation in four studies:

> In the initial *transfer study*, physically healthy and psychologically robust elderly women were studied when they were forced to move from a small, hotel-like institution to a larger, quasi-military institution for the aged. In the *institutionalization study*, community-dwelling aged persons were studied as they voluntarily entered homes for the aged, to meet physical or social needs. In the *therapeutic transfer study*, a highly selected group of geriatric patients were studied as they were prepared for discharge from a mental hospital to a variety of community-based institutional and semi-institutional settings. The *mass transfer study*, finally, examined 470 geriatric patients who were relocated en masse from a state mental hospital to a variety of other institutional settings. [Lieberman, 1975, p. 141.]

These studies were longitudinal in design; that is, they included measurements that were taken before the change in residence took place, one year after relocation, and, in some cases, during the transition. The institutionalization and mass transfer studies also included longitudinal examinations of subjects who did not change residences so that adaptive changes of two groups could be compared.

In all four studies, large numbers of subjects (48% to 56%) experienced adaptive failure. In spite of differing individual levels of personal resources, coping techniques, and stress perceptions, the most important predictor of adaptive outcome was the *degree of environmental change* generated by the relocation. In other words, the degree of change was directly related to the degree to which subjects experienced a decline in health or in social or psychological functioning. Consequently, the authors concluded that the critical factor in adaptation to crises is the nature of the stressor itself (the degree to which it disrupts customary behavior patterns), whereas perceptions of stress, personal resources, and coping skills are relatively irrelevant to the adjustment process.

Lieberman and Tobin's perspective is useful for a number of reasons. First, this model clearly reflects the processional nature of adaptation and demonstrates the need for longitudinal data. It is only with longitudinal data that changes over time and changes in function that are directly related to stressors can be discerned. A related strength of the research design is the comparison of adaptive changes between two groups of subjects: one group moved, the other did not. Second, Lieberman and Tobin's model is an appropriately complex one that incorporates subjective as well as objective aspects of social stress and includes an examination of the potential role that personal resources and coping skills play in the adjustment process.

Problems with Lieberman and Tobin's work arise only when their research findings are generalized beyond the types of subjects used in their research. The assumption that personal resources, coping skills, and perceptions of stress are largely irrelevant to adjustment to crises appears premature for several reasons. First, the majority of the subjects used in Lieberman and Tobin's research were physically or psychologically impaired and were facing residential relocation precisely because of those impairments. It's important to note that their samples represent those older people who are most vulnerable to stressful situations and who have the fewest resources to mobilize in response to stress. In addition, since the subjects were responding to a high-impact, pervasive event (an intense crisis rather than a more routine role shift), their relatively high rates of adaptive failure are not surprising. If Lieberman and Tobin had examined life stresses that vary in pervasiveness and intensity and had used a sample that incorporated the entire range of characteristics found among older people, then perceptions of stress, personal resources, and coping skills might have been significant factors in the adaptation process.

Although Lieberman and Tobin's research findings are of limited generalizability, their model of adaptation to crises is a clear illustration of the way in which a variety of relevant concepts can be related and examined in a theoretically meaningful manner. An obvious need for future research is the application of Lieberman and Tobin's model to broader samples of older people, experiencing a variety of life stresses.

Labeling and Social Breakdown in Later Life: Kuypers and Bengtson

Kuypers and Bengtson (1973) are interested in defining the mechanisms that link personal adaptation in old age to structural and normative phenomena in society. They suggest that the *social breakdown syndrome* (SBS), a social labeling theory that was previously proposed as an explanation of mental illness, can further our understanding of the link between self and society in later life.

The essential premise of social labeling theory is that deviance is in the eye of the beholder. *Social labeling theory* reminds us that deviance is a social judgment about particular behaviors, not an inherent property of those behaviors. Therefore, the personal consequences associated with particular behaviors are more closely related to the interpretation and meaning assigned to those behaviors by others than to the behaviors themselves. According to this theory, a deviant is an individual who has been labeled *deviant* by significant or powerful others. Presumably, the deviant has violated normative expectations, but the violation itself doesn't distinguish the deviant from the nondeviant, since some individuals violate the same normative expectations but avoid social labeling. The *labeling process* distinguishes the deviant from the nondeviant. When an individual is labeled *deviant* (or *incompetent, or crazy*), there are two important consequences: first, the label leads to negative sanctions imposed by others; second, since identity is dependent on the treatment we receive from others, the label is likely to lead the individual to define himself or herself as deviant. Finally, the adoption of a deviant identity makes subsequent deviant behavior even more likely.

Figure 4-2 depicts the feedback loop that characterizes the labeling and social breakdown syndrome as they apply to later life. Kuypers and Bengtson argue that role loss, lack of formal socialization procedures, and the termination of normative guidance characteristic of later life constitute a unique and major reorganization process that causes older individuals to be especially susceptible to social labeling. Older people become increasingly dependent on external cues to establish their self-evaluations. Since societal views concerning old age are negative and stereotypic, older people often are treated as if they are incompetent and are negatively labeled, regardless of their personal

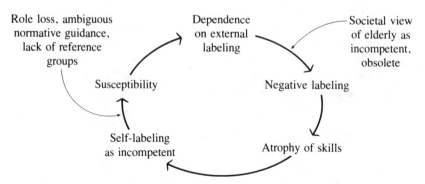

FIGURE 4-2   A systems representation of the social breakdown syndrome as applied to old age. (From "Social Breakdown and Competence," by J. A. Kuypers and V. L. Bengtson, Human Development, *1973, 16, 190. Reprinted by permission.)*

characteristics. Older persons often internalize these negative social evaluations, experience an actual decline in competence, and label themselves negatively. The feedback loop is completed as this negative self-evaluation causes older individuals to be more vulnerable to negative labeling.

Kuypers and Bengtson use the term *competence* in much the same way I use the term *adjustment,* suggesting that it includes both objective and subjective components. They identify three major dimensions of competence: effective role performance, the ability to cope, and a sense of mastery. Since the SBS has a negative impact on the skills and identities of older people, all three dimensions of competence are likely to decline in later life.

The SBS perspective helps us to understand social adjustment in later life by linking the personal well-being of older persons to structural and normative conditions in society. Moreover, the description of the model as a feedback loop sensitizes us to the fact that social adjustment is a dynamic process.

SBS raises both theoretical and empirical problems. First, like Lieberman and Tobin's research on adaptation to crises, SBS theory incorporates a view of the elderly as vulnerable victims of a hostile environment. Undoubtedly this explains, in part, why the SBS model doesn't include explicit recognition of the importance of personal resources or coping skills. Although the authors state that negative personal outcomes are not inevitable and that "the roots of individual variation must be explored" (Kuypers & Bengtson, 1973, [p. 192]), they appear to believe that atrophy of skills and the development of negative self-evaluations are the most likely outcomes. The SBS perspective leaves little room for believing that old age can offer welcome relief from former responsibilities and new opportunities to pursue a lifestyle based on personal preferences.

Available evidence suggests that negative self-evaluation in later life is the exception rather than the rule. As I noted in Chapter 3, evidence suggests that most older people are well-adjusted—that they meet the demands of their environments and report satisfactory levels of personal well-being—and maintain a positive sense of self. Therefore, although SBS might describe self-identification as incompetent for some older people, it doesn't appear to describe the typical pattern of adjustment to role transitions in later life.

Socialization to Old Age: Rosow

Rosow's efforts to conceptualize adult socialization, especially socialization to old age, span nearly two decades. A review of his works provides an intriguing glimpse of one sociologist's attempts to identify and refine the major issues regarding socialization in later life.

Rosow's first paper regarding adult socialization (1965) explored the consequences of imperfect socialization for social systems. This focus on systems rather than on individuals is characteristic of Rosow's work and reflects his ties to structural sociological perspectives. He begins with the premise that successful socialization has two components: (1) conformity to behavioral role expectations, and (2) internalization of the beliefs and values that relate to a particular role. He then developed a classification system of four socialization types (see Figure 4-3). The typology includes successful socialization—behavioral conformity and internalization of appropriate values—and three types of individuals who exhibit imperfect socialization: dilettantes, chameleons, and unsocialized individuals. Dilettantes successfully internalize appropriate values, but they don't conform to behavioral expectations. Chameleons, on the other hand, conform to behavioral expectations, but they fail to internalize appropriate values. Finally, the unsocialized individual is deficient in both behavior and values.

Rosow argues that, from the perspective of the social system, dilettantes and chameleons present the most problems. Socialized individuals are obviously the desired type. Unsocialized individuals are of little benefit to a system, but they are identifiable and can be sanctioned or forced to relinquish their roles. Under normal conditions, chameleons are useful, because their behavior contributes to the ongoing operations of a social system. Conversely, under routine conditions, dilettantes aren't very useful. Although they internalize appropriate values, they fail to conform to behavioral expectations. Under conditions of stress, however, the relative advantages of dilettantes and chameleons are reversed (see Figure 4-3). Since chameleons have no commitment to the underlying values of a social system, they find it relatively easy to allow behavioral expectations to lapse in times of stress. Dilettantes, on the other hand, maintain belief in appropriate values and can be of benefit to a social system during times of stress. Until times of stress or adversity arise, it is often impossible to distinguish between the socialized individual and the chameleon, since, under routine conditions, both exhibit behavioral conformity.

| Socialization Types | Adoption of: | | Rank Order of Effectiveness: | |
	Values	Behavior	Routine Conditions	Stressful Conditions
Socialized	+	+	1	1
Dilettante	+	−	3	2
Chameleon	−	+	2	3
Unsocialized	−	−	4	4

FIGURE 4-3 Forms of socialization and their effectiveness under routine and stressful conditions. (Reprinted with permission from Social Forces, September 1965, 44, 35–45. "Forms and Functions of Adult Socialization," by I. Rosow. Copyright © The University of North Carolina Press.)

Rosow then turned his attention to the specific issues of status, role, and socialization in old age (Rosow, 1973). He argued that the role losses which commonly occur in later life create crises for older people. Role losses experienced in later life have a number of unique features. First, role loss excludes the aged from significant participation in many areas of social life, thereby devaluing them. Second, role loss in later life occurs systematically to the entire older population; it isn't based on each individual's role performance. Third, because our society doesn't prepare individuals to assume a viable role in later life, many older persons experience loss of social identity. Individual adaptation to old age is highly dependent on personal tolerance of stress and the availability of social support networks.

In *Socialization to Old Age* (1974), Rosow maintains that old age is a vague and devalued status that lacks clear behavioral guidelines and effective socialization mechanisms. He suggests that research has failed to find a well-defined, shared social role of "older person." Moreover, research suggests that a substantial proportion of older people don't think of themselves, or at least will not admit that they think of themselves, as old. Therefore, Rosow contends, neither component of successful socialization exists in relation to the role of older person—there are no clear guidelines by which to teach or evaluate behavioral conformity and self-identification as an older person is relatively rare.

In 1976, Rosow returned to an examination of the concepts of status and role. Rosow argues that status and role can best be viewed as independent phenomena—a distinction with important consequences for the social position of older people. With this perspective, he developed a four-part typology (see Figure 4-4). According to this typology, an *institutional role pattern* exists when a social status is accompanied by a specific, identifiable role. This role pattern is the one addressed by traditional role theory. A *tenuous role pattern* exists when a social status is not accompanied by a well-defined role. An *informal role pattern* is characterized by the development of a social role in the absence of a publicly-defined social status. The fourth possibility, which is

Role Types	Status	Role
Institutional	+	+
Tenuous	+	−
Informal	−	+
Nonrole	−	−

FIGURE 4-4   Rosow's status-role typology. *(From "Status and Role Change Through the Life Span," by I. Rosow. In R. H. Binstock and E. Shanas [Eds.],* Handbook of Aging and the Social Sciences. *Copyright © 1976 by Litton Educational Publishing, Inc. Reprinted by permission of Van Nostrand Reinhold Company.)*

a logical but theoretically irrelevant pattern, is the nonrole, or the absence of both status and role.

Rosow argues that old age is a tenuous role pattern. Although he views old age as an identifiable social status, he finds no evidence of a shared, identifiable configuration of behavioral expectations that accompany that status. Since old age is a status without a role, there cannot be effective socialization mechanisms to prepare people for old age. The loss of social identity Rosow believes to be characteristic of old age results from an age-related loss of institutional roles and the fact that the newly acquired status of older person lacks a viable behavioral component.

The relationship between social structure and personal well-being in later life has been a dominant theme of Rosow's work, contributing to our understanding of the problems that social structure can generate for older people. Rosow's work is particularly effective in describing the ways in which the larger social structure influences the social position of the older population: the predictable loss of meaningful social roles, the exclusion of older people from valued social institutions, and the consequent devaluation of later life. In spite of his contributions, a number of Rosow's conclusions are overgeneralized and premature.

First, Rosow's contention that personal well-being depends on active participation in significant numbers of what he terms *institutional role patterns* appears somewhat premature. If, indeed, the status of older person lacks explicit behavioral expectations, that doesn't necessarily imply that later life involves loss of personal identity. It is possible that informal role patterns (such as leisure roles) become increasingly significant in late adulthood. The opportunity to develop informal roles that are based on lifestyle preferences might even be welcomed by older people. This issue merits further systematic research.

Second, as is true of the models of Lieberman and Tobin and Kuypers and Bengtson, a crisis orientation is central to Rosow's perspective: older people are victims of a society which is indifferent at best and hostile at worst. Identity is threatened and anomie a risk in a society that excludes older people from meaningful, institutional roles. This generalization simply is not compatible with the compelling accumulation of empirical evidence that the vast majority of older persons meet the demands of their environments and report at least moderate levels of life satisfaction. This does not deny the fact that the social structure does generate problems for some older people. What must be avoided, however, is an overly deterministic view of the impact of such structural arrangements upon personal well-being during late life.

Rosow's unit of analysis is different from the focus of this book: he is primarily interested in delineating broad social patterns, whereas this book emphasizes the factors that affect the social adjustment and identities of individuals. Rosow asks important sociological questions, and his answers are thoughtful expositions of a structural perspective. Although his conclusions serve as a useful description of the structural context of later life for our purposes, a theoretical perspective that will enable us to understand the conditions under which late life is experienced as enriching or debilitating also is needed.

Intentionality across the Life Cycle: Lowenthal, Thurnher, and Chiriboga

Lowenthal and her colleagues have focused on the issues of social stress, adaptation, and psychological well-being in later life. The works reviewed here are part of a recent study of stress and adaptation at four different life stages.

Lowenthal and her associates define *adaptation* as goodness of fit between ends and means (Lowenthal, 1971; Lowenthal & Chiriboga, 1973; Lowentha, Thurnher, & Chiriboga, 1975). Intentionality—an individual's adaptive process—consists of personal efforts to make goals and behavior compatible. An adapted individual is able to maintain congruity between goals and behavior, whereas an unadapted person experiences a significant discrepancy between values and behavior. Social stress is experienced in situations that preclude or threaten the fit between goals and behavior. The impact of typical life events or normative transitions associated with various life stages is particularly important.

Lowenthal et al. carefully distinguish between objective conditions conducive to stress, which they label *presumed stress,* and individual perceptions of stress. Using a four-cell table, they developed a typology of conditions that reflects the relationship between presumed stress and perceptions of stress (see Figure 4-5). According to this typology, people are either lucky, challenged, self-defeating, or overwhelmed. Lucky individuals neither experience nor perceive much stress. Challenged individuals are exposed to significant amounts of stress, but they don't perceive themselves as stressed. Self-defeating individuals perceive a great deal of stress, even though they are exposed to relatively small amounts of objective stress. Finally, overwhelmed individuals both experience and perceive relatively large amounts of stress. This simple typology illustrates the possible relationships between objective stress indicators and subjective perceptions of stress.

An individual's general adaptive status is viewed as the relationship between deficits (problems, stresses) and resources. In addition to physical health, five psychological characteristics are important resources: accommodation, growth (openness to new experience), hope, mutuality (the ability to develop and sustain meaningful and supportive interpersonal relationships), and intelligence. In other words, resources (as defined by Lowenthal and her associates) are similar to the personal characteristics we have termed *coping skills.*

Presumed Stress:	Preoccupation with Stress:	
	Low	High
Frequent and/or Severe	Challenged	Overwhelmed
Infrequent and/or Mild	Lucky	Self-defeating

FIGURE 4-5 Stress typology of Lowenthal, Thurnher, and Chiriboga. (From Four Stages of Life, by M. F. Lowenthal, M. Thurnher, and D. Chiriboga. Copyright 1975 by Jossey-Bass, Inc., Publishers. Reprinted by permission.)

Following Bradburn's (1969) lead of independently assessing negative and positive feelings, Lowenthal et al. developed a four-category affect typology (see Figure 4-6). According to this typology, bland individuals report little affect of either a positive or negative tone, exultant persons report a predominance of positive feelings, beset individuals report a preponderance of negative feelings, and volatile individuals experience large amounts of both positive and negative feelings. The advantage of this classification system is that it permits an assessment of both the quality (positive versus negative) and the quantity of affect. Levels of affect can then be compared to the balance between resources and deficits in order to determine the adaptive status that is closely related to a subjective sense of well-being.

In Four Stages of Life (Lowenthal et al., 1975), social stress, adaptation, and psychological well-being of various life-stage groups were examined and compared. The comparisons were based on life stage rather than chronological age, because Lowenthal et al. hypothesized that the social demands of each life stage, rather than age itself, account for significant differences in stress and adaptation across the life course. The sample in their study was made up of men and women who faced normative life events at four different life stages: (1) high school seniors, who faced occupational, familial, and residential changes; (2) newlyweds, who were assuming marital roles and facing childbearing decisions; (3) middle-aged persons, who were experienc-

Number of Negative Feelings:	Number of Positive Feelings:	
	Low	High
Low	Bland	Exultant
High	Beset	Volatile

FIGURE 4-6 Affect typology of Lowenthal, Thurnher, and Chiriboga. (Adapted from Four Stages of Life, by M. F. Lowenthal, M. Thurnher, and D. Chiriboga. Copyright 1975 by Jossey-Bass, Inc., Publishers. Reprinted by permission of the authors and publisher.)

ing peak career demands and facing the departure of the last child from the home; and (4) older workers (or their spouses), who were anticipating departure from the labor market.

The results of this study are intriguing and complex. Apparently, both gender and life stage are related to stress, adaptation, and resources. If we apply the stress typology described earlier (see Figure 4-5) to high school seniors and newlyweds, the results suggest that women are more likely to be lucky or challenged, whereas men are more frequently rated as self-defeated or overwhelmed. Among middle-aged participants and older workers, this pattern was reversed: women were more frequently described as overwhelmed or self-defeated, whereas men were more likely to be lucky or challenged. These findings suggest that earlier life stages are more stressful for men, whereas later life stages take a more severe toll on women.

The results also indicated that volatile individuals were largely found among high school seniors and newlyweds. Bland persons were usually older workers, and beset individuals were most frequently middle-aged. The few exultant individuals identified in the study were newlyweds or older workers.

Finally, examination of the relationship between affect and levels of resources and deficits also yielded interesting life-stage differences. Among high school seniors, the happiest individuals were those who had the highest levels of both resources and deficits. The happiest newlyweds reported high levels of resources and low levels of deficits. The happiest middle-aged respondents reported intermediate levels of resource and low levels of deficits. Among the older workers, the happiest individuals reported low levels of resources and deficits. This pattern suggests that a personal sense of well-being may be dependent on greater levels of complexity in young adulthood than at later life stages.

Each stage of life apparently has its unique problems. High school seniors, newlyweds, middle-aged persons, and older workers all confront significant life events or role transitions that require negotiation and adaptation. In spite of this, each life stage is experienced by a majority of study participants as pleasant. All stages of adulthood, it appears, have satisfying and enriching aspects.

The work of Lowenthal and her associates provides an intriguing perspective of stress and adaptation across the life course. One of their most interesting conclusions is the notion that conditions that are conducive to social adjustment differ from one life stage to another. This theme repeatedly emerges in *Four Stages of Life,* where, for example, it is suggested that the experience of multiple life events has a positive impact during earlier life stages but creates stress during later stages of adulthood. Similarly, psychological and affective complexity is viewed as a correlate of positive adjustment in early life stages, whereas middle-aged persons and older workers are reported to be better off with relatively simple configurations of psychological resources and affective states. If, in future research, these patterns can be replicated with the use of longitudinal data, a major link will be established between developmental processes inherent to the organism and external environmental conditions. Although the life-course perspective is valuable, all available research findings are based on cross-sectional data. Until longitudinal data are available, observed life-stage differences must be cautiously interpreted. At this point, we don't know whether observed life stage differences reflect the impact of stage-specific social patterns or differences among historically unique cohorts.

Lowenthal et al.'s research appears to lack an explicit underlying model. Although she and her associates describe and examine a variety of meaningful concepts, one is often unsure of how the concepts are used or how they are expected to interrelate. The researchers recognize this fact, asserting that "any stress-adaptation paradigm will have some components whose placement in one or another parameter is arbitrary" (Lowenthal & Chiriboga, 1973, p. 289). Unfortunately, when research efforts are not guided by a precise model, interpretation of results is confusing. Therefore, although Lowenthal et al.'s work is useful, it would be aided by a more explicit model of stress and adaptation.

An Integrated Model
of Social Adjustment

In this section, an integrated model for understanding and empirically examining social stress, especially role transitions, will be introduced. The model, which is intended to specify the relationships among relevant concepts, is empirically testable and will guide interpretations of research results. In addition, the model explicitly incorporates recognition of the individual's capacity to actively respond to stressful situations. It is especially valuable in that it will help us to understand the conditions under which presumed stressful situations are or are not experienced as stressful and, therefore, do or do not lead to negative outcomes.

The model, which was developed by House (1974), includes five major classes of variables:

> (1) *objective social conditions* conducive to stress; (2) individual *perceptions of stress;* (3) individual *responses* (physiological, affective, and behavioral) to perceived stress; (4) more enduring *outcomes* of perceived stress and responses thereto; and (5) individual and situational *conditioning variables* that specify the relationships among the first four sets of factors. [House, 1974, p. 13].

Figure 4-7 illustrates House's model, which interrelates these five classes of variables. The solid lines between the boxes represent hypothesized causal directions, and the broken lines stemming from the box labeled *Conditioning Variables* indicate that individual and situational factors condition or affect the relationships among other variables.

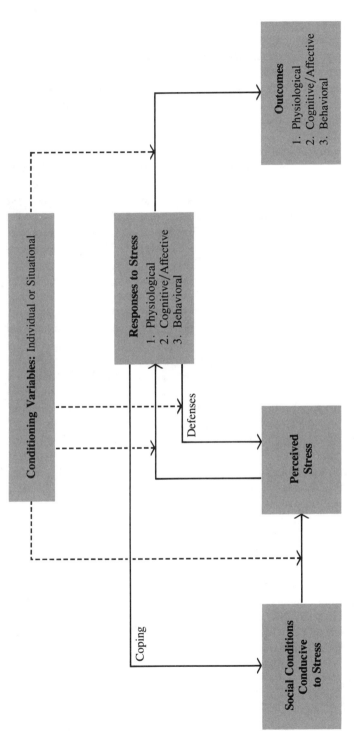

FIGURE 4-7 House's model of social stress. (From "Occupational Stress and Coronary Heart Disease: A Review and Theoretical Integration," by J. S. House, Journal of Health and Social Behavior, 1974, 15, 13. Copyright 1974 by the American Sociological Association. Reprinted by permission of the author and publisher.)

The model begins with specification of the presumed stressor, which influences an individual's perception of a situation. If the presumed stressor is not perceived as problematic, stress responses will not occur. The model accommodates such a possibility by indicating that the relationship between objective conditions and personal perceptions is influenced by individual or situational variables. For example, access to sufficient resources could help an individual to deal with objective conditions conducive to stress without viewing them as stressful.

Perceptions of stress trigger responses at various levels (physiological, psychological, and behavioral) and undoubtedly vary from one individual to another; that is, people react differently to the same objective situations. In addition, individual and situational factors influence an individual's response to stress. House (1974) has employed the distinction, made in previous works, between coping and defense. Coping is directed toward modifying the objective conditions that are conducive to stress, whereas defense refers to alteration of stress perception.

Finally, the effects, or long-term consequences, of stress are tapped by a relevant outcome measure. Choice of an appropriate outcome measure is determined by the research question and the nature of the stress. Like other parts of the model, outcomes can be influenced by individual or situational variables.

The processual nature of stress and adjustment are clearly incorporated into the model. The only important element that is missing from the model is a baseline measure of the appropriate outcome variable. In order to link a change in status to the impact of the stressor, it's necessary to compare the outcome measure to an individual's status prior to stress.

Figure 4-8 illustrates a slightly modified version of House's model. First, a baseline measure of the individual's status prior to stress has been added. Second, although House's labels have been retained, the concepts that are relevant to social adjustment in later life have been appropriately placed in the model. Role transitions and role shifts are listed as conditions that are conducive to stress; perceptions of role transitions and shifts as stressful reflect the subjective experience of loss, or anomie; personal resources, coping skills, and socialization experiences are important conditioning variables; and social adjustment and identity are the outcome variables of interest. The model also indicates that conditioning variables can affect situations conducive to stress. For example, preventive coping, or appropriate socialization experiences, can prevent the occurrence of stressful situations.

In summary, House's model of the social stress paradigm suits our needs. The model relates relevant concepts, it is empirically testable, and it provides a framework for the interpretation of research findings. In addition, it clearly incorporates the processual nature of stress and adjustment and recognizes individual capacity to actively respond to stressful situations. House suggests that his model is "presented as a heuristic device for clarifying and integrating existing research and suggesting critical areas for further research"

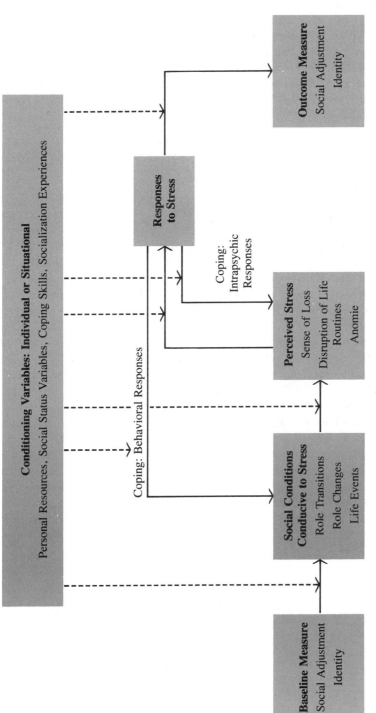

FIGURE 4-8   Modified version of House's social stress model.

(1974, p. 15). In the remaining chapters of this book, House's model, as it is depicted in Figure 4-8, will be used to clarify existing research that focuses on the major role transitions and role changes of later life. Such a review is intended to increase our understanding of adjustment to specific role transitions and, more importantly, to demonstrate that we can understand the major discontinuities of later life by using a conceptual model based on the social stress paradigm.

Review Questions

1. *What is the role of coping behavior in the models of: (1) Lieberman and Tobin, (2) Kuypers and Bengtson, (3) Rosow, and (4) Lowenthal, Thurnher, and Chiriboga?*
2. *Lieberman and Tobin developed their model of adaptation to life crises by studying the process and effects of institutionalization. Lowenthal, Thurnher, and Chiriboga developed their stress model by studying pre-retirees and young adults. In what ways do the conclusions of these two research teams reflect the characteristics of the samples used in their research efforts?*
3. *What are conditioning variables? Why are they important in the study of adjustment to role transitions in later life?*
4. *Kuypers and Bengtson posit that the role losses and dependencies characteristic of later life make older people especially dependent on external cues provided by others. They suggest that this dependence on external cues increases the likelihood of self-labeling as incompetent. Is it possible that this dependency on external cues could be used to facilitate feelings of personal efficacy or self-worth? Why, or why not?*
5. *One of the advantages of the models developed by Kuypers and Bengtson and by Rosow is an explicit recognition of the importance of the social structure for personal well-being in later life. In what ways are the effects of social structure on individual well-being implicit in the models of Lieberman and Tobin, Lowenthal and her associates, and House?*

5

Role Transitions in Later Life: The World of Work

Retirement is probably one of the most significant role transitions in later life. Most men and a significant and increasing proportion of women are employed outside the home during middle life, and almost all of them will eventually retire; therefore, the number of people involved testifies to the significance of retirement.

Work represents more than a way of making a living. Freud suggested that the major psychosocial tasks of adulthood are to love and to work, and the Protestant Ethic (Weber, 1958) dictates that, indeed, we should love to work. In *Working,* a chronicle of the nature and meaning of work among Americans, Terkel (1972) concludes that work is

> a search, too, for daily meaning as well as daily bread, for recognition as well as cash, for astonishment rather than torpor; in short, for a sort of life rather than a Monday through Friday sort of dying. Perhaps immortality, too, is part of the quest [p. xiii].

Early studies of retirement were based on the assumption that cessation of work is a stressful role transition that leads to a less satisfying lifestyle and the loss of an important source of identity. However, the vast majority of retirees appear to adjust smoothly and with little evidence of trauma. This is not to say that retirement doesn't represent a crisis for some individuals. Rather, the evidence suggests that retirement usually doesn't result in debilitating outcomes. Our task here is to determine the conditions under which retirement is and is not a crisis. In this chapter, our model of adjustment to social stress will be used, in conjunction with existing research findings, to address this issue.

Retirement: Definition and Characteristics

In spite of its common usage, defining the term *retirement* is neither simple nor straightforward. A variety of definitions has been offered, including lack of employment, less than full-time employment, receipt of a retirement pension, and self-description as retired. Often, a specific age span is included in the definition in order to distinguish between retirement and unemployment. Undoubtedly, each of these definitions reflects some aspect of retirement, and each one might help in answering specific research questions; however, for our purposes, we need a general and meaningful definition, such as Atchley's (1976):

> Retirement is a condition in which an individual is . . . employed less than full-time . . . and in which his income is derived at least in part from a retirement pension earned through prior years of service as a job holder. Both of these conditions must be met for an individual to be retired [p. 1].

According to this definition, which maintains a distinction between the retired and the unemployed, retirement is restricted to persons who are at the end of their occupational careers.

Retirement can be viewed as an *event,* a *role,* or a *process*—and, in fact, it is all of these. As an *event,* retirement marks the end of a person's work life and is often accompanied by formal recognition (parties and the publicly acknowledged "last day of work"). The symbolism and subjective meaning of retirement as an event is a rich and largely unexamined area of study, but a focus on the retirement event per se has two major limitations. First, many retired persons never experience a retirement event. For example, an unemployed older person who finally becomes eligible for a retirement pension quietly ceases to be unemployed and becomes retired (without a formal retirement event). Second, the retirement event doesn't encompass much of the significance that retirement holds for an individual: retirement, obviously, is more than an occasion.

When it is viewed as a *role,* retirement refers to the behavioral expectations—the rights and duties—of retirees. Retirement has been described as a "roleless role," which implies an absence of behavioral guidelines. From this perspective, retirement is viewed as an example of Rosow's tenuous role pattern—a status without a role. Contrary to this perspective, Atchley has argued that "Being a retired person is a definite position in American society, and there is widespread agreement concerning what kind of behavior to expect from retired people" (1976, p. 4). He suggests that the rights of retirees include: (1) economic support without a job and without negative social evaluation, and (2) autonomous management of personal time. Their responsibilities include: (1) managing their personal lives without assistance, and (2) making appropriate lifestyle decisions. In general, then, although the role of retiree is more flexible and informal than many other roles, retirement can be viewed as a social role.

Finally, retirement is a *process* in which an individual's career is ended or curtailed—a process in which the consequences of retirement (such as loss of income and increase in free time) are recognized, negotiated, and resolved. Atchley (1976) views retirement as both a role and a process. He describes two phases that precede the retirement event and five phases that follow the cessation of work (see Figure 5-1). The pre-retirement phases, especially the Near Phase, are characterized by anticipation of and planning for retirement, although the scope and depth of planning varies widely among individuals. After the retirement event, initial feelings of relief and freedom generate a Honeymoon Phase, during which the individual views retirement as an endless vista of opportunity. The Disenchantment Phase is a period of emotional letdown that is experienced as the realities of retirement, some of which are negative, are acknowledged. During the Reorientation Phase, the realities of retirement are negotiated. The subsequent resolution generates a Stability Phase, during which the basic routine of retirement lifestyle is implemented. Finally, during the Termination Phase, the individual relinquishes the role of retired person. In some cases, the role is lost because of death; in others, a new role (for example, institutionalized person) is taken. Unfortunately, it appears that this model is untestable, since, as Atchley informs us: (1) not everyone experiences every phase, (2) the order of the phases varies among individuals, and (3) the phases aren't tied to chronological age or other measures of time. These qualifications make it impossible to support or refute the proposed model. In spite of this, Atchley raises the issue of process and sensitizes us to the fact that long-term retirees experience different circumstances than recent retirees.

Now we will turn to a consideration of retirement from a social stress perspective. Each major category of the stress model will be reviewed and specified on the basis of previous research findings.

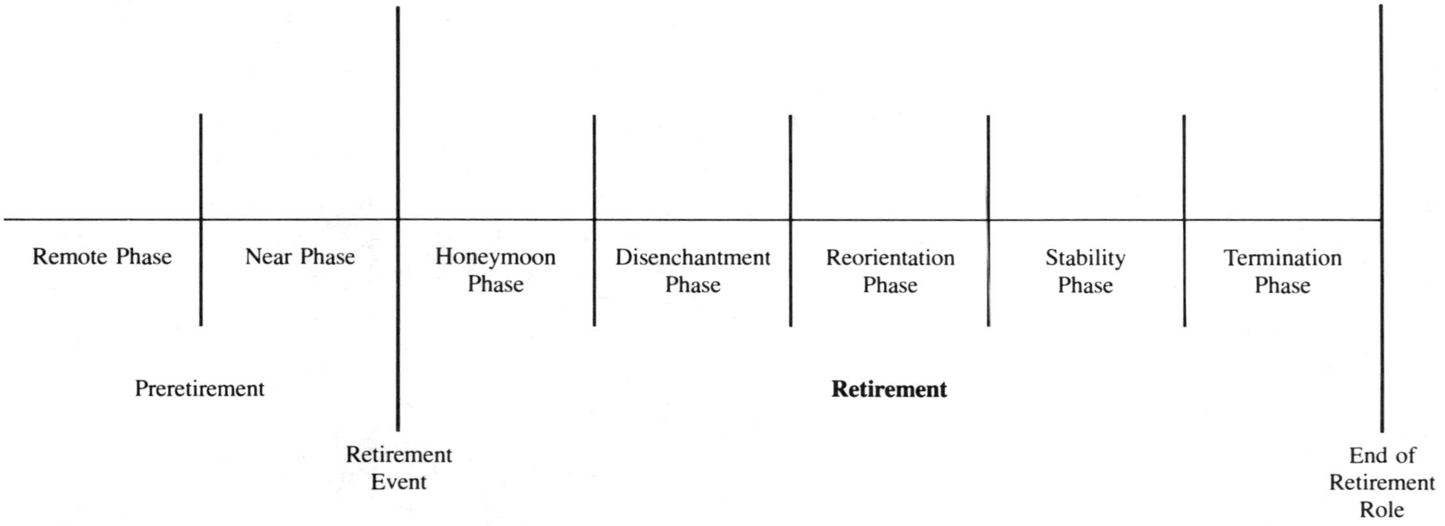

Remote Phase	Near Phase	Honeymoon Phase	Disenchantment Phase	Reorientation Phase	Stability Phase	Termination Phase

Preretirement

Retirement Event

Retirement

End of Retirement Role

FIGURE 5-1 Atchley's hypothesized phases of retirement. (From The Sociology of Retirement, by R. C. Atchley. Copyright 1976 by Schenkman Publishing Company. Reprinted by permission.)

Does Retirement
Contribute to Stress?

In early studies of retirement, many theorists argued strongly that, because of the significance of work in the adult life cycle, retirement poses a major adaptive challenge for older individuals. In a classic study, Friedmann and Havighurst (1954) developed a five-part typology of the meanings of work. First (and most obvious), work is a source of income. Second, work can provide a life routine that structures the use of time. Third, work can be a major source of personal status and identity. Fourth, work often functions as a context in which meaningful social interaction can take place—work peers often are friends. Finally, work can be a source of meaningful experience—an arena in which individuals serve society, express creativity, and obtain the intrinsic satisfactions of accomplishment. Friedmann and Havighurst argue that individuals can find any or all of these elements in their work, and that, to the degree that these elements are no longer available after retirement, individuals experience a sense of loss. Perceptions of stress in retirement are determined by the nature of the perceived loss and an individual's ability to find alternate, or substitute, sources of meaning. For example, individuals who view their work primarily as a source of income will probably find retirement stressful if financial resources are scarce, but they might not find retirement stressful if they have adequate incomes.

Attitudes Toward
Retirement

Work orientation refers to an individual's attitude toward work. It includes work commitment, the intrinsic satisfactions of work, and general job satisfaction. Numerous studies have examined work orientation among older workers and retirees. In general, older employees report higher levels of job satisfaction than younger workers (see Sheppard & Philibert, 1972; Wright & Hamilton, 1978). These results could reflect differences among cohorts, but most evidence suggests that higher levels of job satisfaction reflect (1) the fact that many older workers are long-term employees who have earned seniority and status within their occupation, or (2) the fact that older workers may have changed jobs several times before finding a satisfying position (Wright & Hamilton, 1978). In spite of this, most retired persons (Simpson, Back, & McKinney, 1966b), as well as a large proportion of older workers (Fillenbaum, 1971; Goudy, Powers, & Keith, 1975a; 1975b), report low levels of work orientation. For these individuals, retirement wouldn't be perceived as a loss of meaningful life experience. As we will see, a variety of conditioning variables help to explain the kinds of older persons who report high work orientation.

Attitudes toward retirement among both retirees and older workers have been examined in numerous studies. In all of these studies, a significant proportion of the respondents reported positive attitudes toward retirement, with a majority of studies reporting that more than 80% of the respondents have positive attitudes toward retirement (Friedmann & Havighurst, 1954; Gernant, 1972; Kell & Patton, 1978; Streib & Schneider, 1971).

We might expect those persons who are most satisfied with and committed to their jobs to have the most negative attitudes toward retirement; however, available evidence doesn't support this assumption. Many studies have found no relationship between attitudes toward work and attitudes toward retirement (see Fillenbaum, 1971; Goudy, Powers, & Keith, 1975a; 1975b; Johnson & Strouther, 1962). As Seltzer and Atchley (1971) conclude, "It is apparently possible for people to be highly committed toward their profession and at the same time have other things that they might like to do as well" (p. 16).

Other kinds of information provide evidence that suggests retirement is not typically perceived as stressful. First, it has frequently been suggested that mandatory retirement is likely to be more stressful than voluntary retirement. Although it seems logical that an imposed event would be more difficult to cope with than a chosen role transition, there is little evidence that forced retirement poses problems for many older people. Perhaps the knowledge that the work role will be relinquished at a specified age enables people to prepare for retirement. If an individual deeply values work, then mandatory retirement could be distasteful. In fact, under these circumstances, retirement has been related to lower levels of life satisfaction (Kimmel, Price, & Walker, 1978; Thompson, Streib, & Kosa, 1960). The important point here is that these conditions apparently apply to very few older persons. The vast majority of retired persons voluntarily relinquish their work roles, which suggests that retirement isn't typically perceived as a dreaded crisis.

Second, early retirement is becoming an increasingly common phenomenon. For example, in a recent longitudinal study of retirement, 17% of the men age 58–63 were retired. Two years later, 32% had retired (Fillenbaum, 1979). Two primary factors were related to the decision to retire early: poor health and the availability of a retirement pension (Schwab, 1977). Although some individuals are in such poor health that early retirement is virtually a necessity, many healthy individuals welcome the opportunity to quit work. For example, in a study of automobile workers who received the option of an early retirement pension as part of a collective bargaining agreement, many workers retired early (for reasons unrelated to health) and adjusted to the loss of the work role (Barfield & Morgan, 1969). A recent study of college professors—an occupational group typically described as highly work oriented and unlikely to retire—demonstrated that with sufficient incentives, typically adequate financial arrangements, early retirement is often viewed as acceptable and highly attractive (Kell & Patton, 1978). The increasing numbers of older workers who opt for early retirement testify to the fact that retirement isn't generally viewed as crisis.

In summary, then, although work provides a variety of important elements in life, most people apparently look forward to retirement, including those people who are most committed to and satisfied with their occupations. In the next section, we will examine the impact of retirement on identity and adjustment.

The Impact of Retirement on Adjustment and Identity

If retirement constitutes a crisis, we would expect to see declines in adjustment or negative impacts on identity as a result of retirement. Unquestionably, retirement signifies a change in customary behavior patterns. Consequently, negotiations and changes in lifestyle are unavoidable. But what is the degree of impact? Are these lifestyle changes easily accomplished? Does adjustment to retirement require major reorientation with a significant risk of negative outcomes?

Social Adjustment. Available evidence clearly indicates that most retirees are well-adjusted (see Atchley, 1976; George & Maddox, 1977; Thompson, Streib, & Kosa, 1960; Streib & Schneider, 1971). In other words, most retirees meet the demands of their environments and are satisfied with their lives. Some studies of retirees are based on cross-sectional data that compare retired persons to older individuals who remain in the labor market (Simpson, Back, & McKinney, 1966b; Kell & Patton, 1978; Atchley, 1971), whereas others are based on longitudinal data that reflect observations of change over a period of time (George & Maddox, 1977; Streib & Schneider, 1971). These studies suggest that, although some individuals experience declines in adjustment after retirement, the predominant pattern is one of consistently adequate adjustment.

Identity. Several aspects of the self are related to retirement, but to a very limited extent. Back and Guptill (1966) examined three dimensions of self-rating among retired and older working men: involvement, optimism, and autonomy. The results of their study indicated that, although retirement had little effect on self-ratings of optimism and autonomy, the retirees scored significantly lower on involvement than the older workers.

Job deprivation, or missing some aspect of work other than income, has been examined in several studies (Cottrell & Atchley, 1969; Fillenbaum, 1971; Simpson, Back, & McKinney, 1966a; Streib & Schneider, 1971). Results of these studies indicate that a majority of the respondents experienced very low levels of job deprivation. Cottrell and Atchley also report that their sample of retired school teachers and telephone company employees is characterized by high levels of self-esteem. Finally, Streib and Schneider report a small retirement-related decline in feelings of usefulness. Apparently, self-ratings of instrumentality—usefulness, or involvement—are related to the impact of retirement, whereas more global assessments of identity are unaffected by retirement. Retirement *does* pose an identity threat to some individuals, but the general pattern appears to be one of continuity in personal levels of self-esteem, self-concept, and identity.

Conditioning Variables: Determining When Retirement Is and Is Not Stressful

Up to this point, general patterns of adjustment to retirement have been described. It appears that a majority of retirees are well-adjusted individuals who don't experience major identity threats as a consequence of retirement or perceive retirement as stressful. Although familiarity with this basic pattern is useful, it is also important to understand the conditions under which retirement is and is not experienced as stressful. Examination of conditioning, or mediating, variables helps us to better understand these complexities. Research suggests four important types of conditioning variables that affect adjustment to retirement: social status variables, personal resources, personality characteristics related to coping skills, and socialization experiences. Each of these is discussed in the following paragraphs.

Social Status Variables

An individual's location in the social structure is determined by a variety of factors, including occupational status, gender, and marital status. These basic social statuses are pervasive factors in our life experience; therefore, it isn't surprising that these factors influence adjustment to retirement.

Occupational Status. One of the most important factors that affects the retirement process is the type of job from which an individual retires. *Occupational status* refers to the complex configuration of factors associated with occupational prestige. Occupations can be hierarchically ranked on the basis of the prestige associated with a given occupational role. Most authors refer to three broad classes of occupational status: (1) upper-status occupations, which include professional, managerial, and proprietary workers; (2) middle-status occupations, which include craftsmen, skilled workers, sales and clerical workers, and other lower white-collar workers; and (3) lower-status occupations, which include semiskilled and unskilled workers. These occupational groupings represent more than prestige; they also represent differences in education and degree of autonomy.

Occupational status has been related to various components of the retirement process. Occupational status greatly affects the meanings work has for individuals. For example, Simpson, Back, and McKinney (1966b) report that persons with upper-status occupations think about their work primarily in terms of intrinsic satisfactions, the autonomy with which they ply their trade, and the opportunities they have to express themselves. Middle-status and lower-status workers, on the other hand, are more likely to refer to extrinsic factors, including job security, pay, and work-related friendships.

Additional evidence suggests that a worker's *specific* occupation is significantly related to his or her perceptions of the meaning of work. Table 5-1 indicates the percentages of respondents from five occupations who endorse various meanings of work (Friedmann & Havighurst, 1954). The table indicates that a relationship exists between occupational status and the meaning of work, with persons of higher occupational status reporting more intrinsic satisfactions. There are also differences between specific occupations of the same occupational status. For example, although steelworkers and coal miners are of approximately the same occupational status, a significantly greater proportion of coal miners report that their work is meaningful. Therefore, the *specific characteristics* of a job appear to be related to the perception of the meaning of work and could be related to other aspects of the retirement process as well. As Sheppard (1976) recently concluded, "Attitudinal and behavioral data suggest the substantial role played by the nature of the occupa-

TABLE 5-1.   *Meanings of Work for Five Occupations.*

Source of:	Steel Workers	Coal Miners	Sales Personnel	Printers	Physicians
Income	100%	87%	N.R.*	84%	8%
Structured Routine— A Way to Fill Time	34	19	89%	31	18
General Status or Personal Identity	19	17.5	94	50	23
Association (Relationships with Work Peers)	18	19	85	40	23
Meaningful Life Experience	16	27	100	62	56

*Not Reported

From *The Meaning of Work and Retirement*, by E. Friedmann and R. J. Havighurst. Copyright 1954 by the University of Chicago Press. Reprinted by permission.

tion—and within occupation, by specific job-task and skill level—in the retirement decision and perhaps in retirement adjustment" (p. 303).

Occupational status also has been related to the decision to retire (Sheppard, 1976), the age of retirement (Simpson, Back, & McKinney, 1966c; Streib & Schneider, 1971), work orientation (Atchley, 1971; Simpson, Back, & McKinney, 1966b) and life satisfaction, or adjustment, after retirement (George & Maddox, 1977; Simpson, Back, & McKinney, 1966b). The patterns of these relationships indicate that upper-status workers retire at advanced ages, exhibit great levels of work orientation, and report high levels of social adjustment after retirement.

Gender and Marital Status. Until recently, discussions of retirement were based solely on the experiences of men. It is still true that available models of retirement are based largely on the findings of studies of male workers. Although sex differences in retirement patterns are now being examined, available evidence remains scattered, fragmented, and frequently contradictory. For example, although some studies report that women have less positive attitudes toward retirement (Cottrell & Atchley, 1969; Streib & Schneider, 1971), other studies indicate that women are more likely to retire than men (Irelan, Motley, Schwab, Sherman & Murray, 1976; Palmore, 1965). Since these studies use longitudinal data, it's difficult to reconcile these contradictory findings. One possibility is that gender differences reflect differences in marital status. For example, Streib and Schneider report that divorced and widowed women retire significantly later than married and single women. Similarly, Palmore (1965) reported that married women are most likely to retire. On the other hand, it appears that married men are least likely to retire (Irelan et al., 1976; Palmore, 1965).

Sex differences in other retirement-related variables are equally ambiguous. Seltzer and Atchley (1971) report no sex differences in work orientation or disengagement potential (a measure of willingness to retire) in a sample of social workers. Atchley (1971) studied the work orientation of retired men and women from two occupations—teachers and telephone company employees. Compared to the low levels of work orientation exhibited by male and female telephone employees and male teachers, the female teachers, a majority of whom were unmarried, exhibited high levels of work orientation.

Two studies have examined women's adjustment to retirement from a different perspective. Rather than compare male and female retirees, these studies examine three groups of older women: retired women, older employed women, and older homemakers (Fox, 1977; Jaslow, 1976). These studies indicate that, in terms of life satisfaction, or happiness, retired women are less well-adjusted than working women; however, both groups are more satisfied than the homemakers.

Further research is needed to determine the effects of gender and marital status on the retirement process; however, available evidence clearly indicates that both gender and marital status are related to retirement.

Personal Resources

Personal resources play a significant role in adjustment to retirement. Income, health, and social support—three major personal resources—are examined in the following paragraphs.

Income. Since work is a source of income, it isn't surprising that income plays a major role in adjustment to retirement. Indeed, availability of an adequate retirement income is one of the major reasons given for the decision to retire (see Atchley, 1976), especially among workers of lower occupational status (see Sheppard, 1976). The decision to retire early is also closely related to the availability of an adequate retirement income (Barfield & Morgan, 1969; Parnes, Adams, Andrisani, Kohen, & Nestel, 1974), and evidence suggests that even upper-status workers retire early when they are given sufficient economic incentives (Kell & Patton, 1978). Finally, when levels of life satisfaction are reported to be lower among retirees than older workers, much of the difference is directly attributable to levels of income (see Fox, 1977).

Health. Physical well-being is a valuable personal resource. There are some particularly strong relationships between health and other retirement-related variables. First, health often has a direct impact on the retirement decision. A significant proportion of retirees report that poor health was the factor (or one of the factors) that persuaded them to retire (Eisdorfer, 1972; Schwab, 1976; Shanas, 1970). This well-established pattern directly contradicts one of the most prevalent myths about retirement—that people die shortly after they stop working. Available evidence suggests that most individuals who die shortly after they retire were in poor health prior to retirement (Haynes, McMichael & Tyroler, 1978). There is even limited evidence of improvement in physical well-being during retirement (Streib & Schneider, 1971). The results of some studies suggest that poor health hinders adjustment to retirement (George & Maddox, 1977; Streib & Schneider, 1971). In those studies that find lower adjustment (life satisfaction) among retirees than among older workers, much of the difference in levels of adjustment reflects the poorer health of the retirees (Fox, 1977; Thompson, Streib, & Kosa, 1966).

Social Support. Very little detailed information is available concerning the ways in which social support systems affect the process of adjustment to retirement. Research findings suggest that marital status is related to personal well-being during retirement. In particular, married men report significantly higher levels of life satisfaction during retirement than their unmarried peers (see George & Maddox, 1977). However, this relationship between marital status and adjustment during retirement doesn't tell us why the presence of a marital partner contributes to successful adjustment. Certainly we can speculate that the companionship and support provided by a spouse serve as a resource that facilitates feelings of well-being. In spite of this, there is a definite need to know more about the process and the day-to-day negotiations that take place among spouses during retirement.

Further research in the area of social support is clearly needed. We need to know more about the specific types of social support provided by family members as well as the influence of friends and fellow workers on adjustment to retirement.

Personality Characteristics and Coping Skills

Although we have used the term *coping* to refer to behavioral strategies, efforts to alleviate perceptions of stress, and personality predispositions, only the latter have been related to adjustment to retirement. Several authors have suggested that stable personality characteristics are related to patterns of adjustment to retirement. In one classic study (reviewed in Chapter 3), Reichard, Livson, and Peterson (1962) examined patterns of adjustment among retired men. The authors contend that personality characteristics were the most reliable predictors of successful adjustment. The results of their study generated a typology of five personality styles. Those who had mature, rocking chair, or armored styles exhibited successful retirement adjustment, whereas the angry men and the self-haters exhibited less positive adjustment. The authors concluded that the five personality patterns reflect relatively stable coping stances. It's important to note that these results suggest that there are several successful styles of adjustment to retirement.

Gutmann (1972) also suggests a typology of five personality types (in descending order of effectiveness): two active mastery types, two passive mastery types, and one magical mastery type. Promethian-competitive individuals view life as a battle in which the rewards go to those people who fight hardest and with the most cunning. Productive-autonomous individuals emphasize productive achievement and self-reliance. These personality types use an active-mastery orientation, which tends to be the most effective style. Passive mastery includes two types: autoplastic autonomy and syntonic receptivity. Individuals of the first type constrict their life space in order to maintain a sense of control and security. Syntonic receptivity is characterized by denial of aggression and conflict. Magical mastery, the least effective personality style, is characterized by denial and projection. Unlike Reichard and her associates, Gutmann views these ego-based personality styles as relatively changeable and suggests that they may represent developmental changes. Gutmann maintains that retirement is most stressful for active mastery personality types, because they are most likely to value work and achievement. On the other hand, passive and magical mastery types are more likely to welcome retirement as a relief from instrumental goals. Even if they experience the most stress, however, it's assumed that active mastery personalities would be able to cope most effectively.

Plonk and Pulley (1977) examined the financial-management practices of 50 middle-class couples who had been retired for an average of seven years. The results of their study indicate that 10% of the couples developed written financial plans, 68% maintained mental spending plans, and 22% reported no financial planning. In spite of this wide range in degree of financial planning, 98% of the couples reported that they kept some form of expenditure records. Almost 95% of the couples used credit on a regular basis. During times of increased expenditures, the couples used accumulated assets, worked part-time, or substituted time and skills for monetary expenditures. One-fourth of the sample routinely spent more than their total income, but only three couples reported financial management problems. This study suggests that many older couples cope with reductions in income after retirement, but it also suggests that many of them might not be coping in a way that will ensure long-term financial security.

There is a clear need for further research concerning coping with retirement. We know very little about the behavioral strategies people use to negotiate the transition from worker to retiree and the cognitive strategies they use to alter perceptions of stress during that transition.

Socialization Experiences

Since retirement is usually voluntary, many people take concrete steps in order to prepare for it. In a recent national survey, individuals were asked to evaluate the importance of a number of specific steps that can be taken to prepare for old age (Louis Harris & Associates, 1975). Table 5-2 shows the percentages of persons in two age groups—18 to 64 and 65 and older—who agreed that the steps were important, as well as the percentages of the older group who had actually taken the steps. Although the respondents were reporting endorsements of preparations for old age, many of the steps involved relate to retirement. The results indicate that both younger and older persons believe preparation is important and that, among older respondents, actual preparation usually lags behind endorsement. Of particular relevance is the fact that only a small percentage of respondents endorse retirement preparation programs, and an even smaller percentage of older persons have actually participated in such programs. Several other studies report that relatively few retired persons participate in retirement planning programs (see Davidson & Kunze, 1965; Kalt & Kohn, 1975; Rowe, 1972; Simpson, Back, & McKinney, 1966b). These low participation rates might reflect a lack of interest among potential participants, but it's also possible that they reflect a scarcity of retirement preparation programs. In fact, very few employers offer such programs (see Fritz, 1978; Kalt & Kohn, 1975). Kasschau (1974) points out

TABLE 5-2. *Perceived Importance of Taking Specific Steps to Prepare for Old Age in Two Age Groups and Preparation of Persons Age 65 and Older Who Have Taken Those Steps.*

Step	Percentage of those age 18–64 who think it's a very important step	Percentage of those 65 and over who think it's a very important step	Percentage of those 65 and over who have taken the step
Make sure you'll have medical care available	88	88	88
Prepare a will	82	79	65
Build up your savings	80	85	73
Learn about pension and Social Security benefits	79	85	87
Buy your own home	69	75	74
Develop hobbies and other leisure-time activities	64	61	62
Decide whether you want to move	50	53	72
Plan new part-time or full-time jobs	32	26	16
Talk to older people about what it's like to grow old	24	27	35
Enroll in retirement counseling or preparation programs	23	19	8
Move in with your children or other relatives	5	7	9

Reprinted with permission from *The Myth and Reality of Aging in America*, a study prepared by Louis Harris and Associates, Inc. for The National Council on the Aging, Inc., Washington, D. C. © 1975.

that retirement programs tend to offer one of two orientations: counseling aimed at crises prevention or information that can be used in planning. Available evidence suggests that information provision is the more effective orientation (Glasmer & DeJong, 1975; Kasschau, 1974). Moreover, these programs can provide effective socialization experiences.

Socialization for retirement can be informal or formal. Since most workers plan to retire eventually, anticipatory socialization, or mental rehearsals of what the retirement role will be like, are undoubtedly common. In addition, friends, coworkers, other retired people, the mass media, and other informal sources contribute to socialization during retirement.

Simpson, Back, and McKinney (1966a) examined exposure to various sources of information concerning retirement. A summary of their research findings is presented in Table 5-3. The information was obtained through discussions with retired people, coworkers, company officials, and Social Security personnel, and through reading, listening to radio, and watching television. Comparisons were made on the basis of occupational status (upper, middle, or lower) and retirement status (already retired versus plan to retire). The results are both complex and interesting. First, middle-occupation-status respondents, regardless of retirement status, were more likely than either upper- or lower-occupation status respondents to have received information about retirement. Second, reading about retirement and discussing retirement with coworkers appear to be the most frequently employed means of obtaining information. Finally individuals who were still working had actually received more information about retirement from some sources than had the retired respondents. (The major exceptions to this pattern were discussions with company officials and Social Security personnel. Apparently, these more formal sources of information aren't used until the retirement event is relatively close at hand.)

In summary, formal retirement preparation programs are neither desired by nor available to a majority of older workers. In spite of this, it appears that informal sources of information are used by most individuals when they face retirement.

The Process
of Retirement

Much of the available evidence (and, indeed, many of the findings reported here) are based on cross-sectional studies. In these studies, retired persons are compared with older persons who are still employed. However, in order to understand the process of retirement, we need to examine longitudinal data that lead to an assessment of change over a period of time. Obviously, for our purposes, longitudinal studies should compare individuals' levels of adjustment before and after retirement. In addition, levels of adjustment should

TABLE 5-3. *Percentage of Respondents Receiving Information about Retirement from Six Sources.*

Retirement and Occupational Status	Percentage Who Discusssd with:				Percentage Who Were Exposed to:	
	Retired People	Fellow Workers	Company Officials	Social Security Personnel	Reading Materials about Retirement	TV or Radio Programs about Retirement
Retirees						
Upper Status	15.6	32.5	57.1	15.6	58.4	23.4
Middle Status	34.1	40.7	74.0	44.7	68.3	40.7
Lower Status	21.9	27.6	58.1	26.7	50.5	39.0
Pre-retirees						
Upper Status	29.3	51.2	35.4	8.5	68.3	24.4
Middle Status	55.3	57.9	44.7	5.3	60.5	28.9
Lower Status	23.1	35.9	23.1	0.0	30.8	28.2

From "Exposure to Information On, Preparation For, and Self-Evaluation in Retirement," by I. H. Simpson, K. W. Back, and J. C. McKinney. In I. H. Simpson and J. C. McKinney (Eds.), *Social Aspects of Aging.* Copyright 1966 by Duke University Press. Reprinted by permission.

be monitored over a considerable period of time after retirement. In this way, both the short-term and long-term impact of retirement can be assessed.

Although longitudinal studies of retirement are relatively rare, the available studies provide information concerning retirement as a process. Using life satisfaction as a measure of adjustment, Streib and Schneider (1971) reported that retirement has no apparent impact—either positive or negative—on adjustment. However, when they examined the more specific topic of satisfaction with retirement, Streib and Schneider reported a decrease in satisfaction as time passed—a decrease they attributed to the impact of diminished financial resources.

Stokes and Maddox (1968) and George and Maddox (1977) also used life satisfaction as an indicator of adjustment. According to their studies, patterns of satisfaction are related to the former occupational status of the retiree. Persons who retired from middle- or lower-occupational-status jobs reported declines in satisfaction as time passed; however, individuals of upper-occupational-status reported increases in life satisfaction during retirement.

These studies illustrate the kinds of contributions longitudinal data make to our understanding of the retirement process. Although there are few longitudinal studies available, several major longitudinal studies of retirement are underway (see the Social Security Administration's Longitudinal Retirement History Study; Irelan, et al., 1976). These research projects should add to the base of knowledge regarding retirement as a process.

Adjustment to Retirement: A Summary

The preceding discussion describes our current understanding of adjustment to retirement. In order to assess the usefulness of the social stress model in understanding adjustment to retirement, we need to take the concepts and variables that are related to adjustment to retirement and place them in the social stress model. Figure 5-2 is an illustration of the social stress model as it explains adjustment to retirement.

The social stress model appears to work quite well as a framework for understanding adjustment to retirement. The variety of concepts and variables related to retirement can be applied to various components of the model. The number and variety of conditioning variables identified in the model is especially noteworthy. This range of conditioning variables testifies to the complexity of the retirement process. In sharp contrast to the quantity of conditioning variables is the scarcity of information regarding coping responses, either behavioral or intrapsychic. We simply do not have much information about the cognitive or behavioral strategies individuals use when the retire-

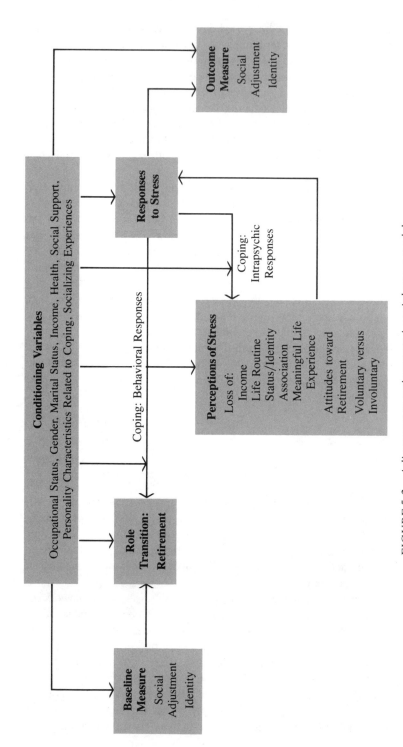

FIGURE 5-2   Adjustment to retirement: A social stress model.

ment process becomes stressful. This demonstrates that the social stress model not only provides a scheme for understanding adjustment to retirement but also highlights the areas in which critical information is still needed.

The most important point here is that the social stress model helps us to understand the conditions under which retirement is and is not likely to lead to negative outcomes. Available evidence suggests that an individual's reaction to retirement is dependent on three types of variables: the degree to which retirement is perceived as stressful, the effectiveness of the coping responses utilized, and the impact of a variety of conditioning variables.

Although information regarding coping responses is incomplete, there are some data concerning personality characteristics related to coping. To simplify somewhat, two groups of individuals are most likely to find the retirement process stressful. The first group consists of individuals who retire from upper-occupational-status jobs. These individuals miss the intrinsic satisfactions derived from work. They are likely to have unfavorable attitudes toward retirement and are least likely to seek relevant socializing experiences. Work was an important source of identity for them. In spite of these factors, upper-occupational-status retirees eventually adjust to retirement. (This can probably be attributed to their relatively comfortable position in terms of personal resources.) The second group consists of lower-occupational-status individuals, who, in spite of the fact that they look forward to retirement, face considerable economic hardship after retirement and tend to be relatively disadvantaged in terms of other resources, such as health and social support.

Finally, it is important to note that available longitudinal studies suggest that, for the most part, retirement appears to have little significant impact on broad levels of social adjustment and identity. Although there is variation, and some individuals do find retirement stressful, continuity in levels of adjustment after retirement is the typical pattern.

Other Work-Related Role Changes and Role Transitions

Although retirement is undoubtedly the most common work-related role shift in later life, others do occur. In the following paragraphs, we will briefly examine two additional work-related role shifts: (1) the change from full-time to part-time work and (2) the return to work after retirement.

Part-Time Work

A shift from full-time to part-time work appears to be an attractive work-related role change for older people, because the retirement process presents less discontinuity when job commitments are gradually relinquished rather than abruptly terminated. Under Social Security guidelines and most retirement programs, limited part-time work has no effect on eligibility for pension benefits. Part-time work provides income, routine, opportunities for interaction, status and identity, and meaningful experiences. The role shift from full-time to part-time worker also has been called *gradual retirement*, which implies that part-time employment is an interim step that eventually leads to *complete retirement*, or total relinquishment of the work role (Schwab, 1977).

Table 5-4 shows the current employment status of adults in the U. S. age 55 and over (Louis Harris & Associates, 1975). The data indicate that fairly small proportions of older individuals are employed part-time. However, after age 65, larger numbers of persons are employed part-time than are employed full-time, which suggests that part-time work is an attractive option for those older persons who wish to continue occupational involvement. In addition, the fact that the 65–69 age group exhibits greatest participation in part-time employment suggests that some older persons use part-time work as a transition phase between full-time employment and complete retirement.

The data in Table 5-4 are cross-sectional; therefore we cannot discern patterns of employment over time. Ideally, we would like to know how many people actually shift from full-time to part-time work in later life. In addition, we would like to know whether those older persons who shift to part-time employment reduce work hours at their full-time jobs or look for new jobs in order to secure part-time work.

Limited longitudinal data that relate to part-time work after retirement have been reported in the Longitudinal Retirement History Study (Schwab, 1977). This national sample included men and unmarried women age 58 to 63 at the first test date. After she examined patterns of complete retirement among men over the first three measurement dates (a 5-year interval), Schwab reported that only 9% of the retirees exhibited gradual retirement—that is,

TABLE 5-4.   *Current Employment Status by Age.*

Employment Status	Percentage by Age			
	55–64	65–69	70–79	80 and Over
Employed Full-Time	38	4	3	1
Employed Part-Time	10	14	8	3
Retired	18	61	63	69
Unemployed	10	4	7	6
Homemaker	22	15	18	20
Other	2	2	1	1

Reprinted with permission from *The Myth and Reality of Aging in America*, a study prepared by Louis Harris and Associates, Inc. for The National Council on the Aging, Inc., Washington, D. C. © 1975.

movement from full-time work to part-time work to no work—whereas 91% reported abrupt retirement—that is, movement from full-time employment to no work.

It isn't clear whether the relatively low rates of part-time work among the elderly reflect a lack of desire for reduced work hours among older workers, structural characteristics of the work place, or both. Observers have noted the scarcity of part-time jobs in our society (see Butler, 1975; Kreps, 1968). If opportunities for part-time work were readily available, more retirees might be attracted to this alternative. Evidence that supports this suggestion comes from two sources. First, in the U.S., self-employed persons, who structure their own work schedules to a greater degree than most workers, often reduce their work hours before they retire (Quinn, 1978; Schwab, 1977). Second, several countries have institutionalized opportunities for part-time work in later life, and these programs have been welcomed by older workers. For example, in Sweden, a National Partial-Pension Scheme was started in 1976. This program permits workers age 60 to 65 to reduce their work hours and collect partial financial support from pensions. The program is being promoted as a preparation for complete retirement (Bratthall, 1976). Norway and Germany have similar programs (Haanes-Olsen, 1974; Wang, 1973). This evidence suggests that older workers find part-time employment attractive.

The shift from full-time to part-time employment in later life is an important topic that deserves further research. We need to know more about individual preferences regarding reduction in work hours, the numbers of older people who are able to reduce their work hours, and the personal characteristics of individuals who choose to work part-time after they retire. In addition, adjustment to part-time work should be examined and compared to adjustment to complete retirement.

Return to Work

The decision to retire is reversible; that is, if a person is unhappy and is physically able to work, it may be possible to relinquish the retirement role and find new employment.

Available evidence suggests that very few individuals return to work after they retire. The Social Security Administration estimates that, within the first three years of retirement, only 8% of retirees return to work. Moreover, 56% of those persons who return to work do so during the first year of retirement (Grad, 1977). These data suggest that very few retirees relinquish their status in favor of the work role. In addition, the pattern of early return to work among those persons who do discard retirement suggests that some older persons who are unemployed but looking for work use retirement benefits as an interim source of support until a job is available. In an earlier longitudinal study of retirement, 17.8% of the women and 19.6% of the men returned to work after they retired (Streib & Schneider, 1971).

Lower-status and upper-status retirees are most likely to return to work (see Fillenbaum & Maddox, 1974; Streib & Schneider, 1971). Lower-status persons who return to work report that their decision was motivated by economic factors. Larger numbers of upper status retirees, especially professionals, return to work, reflecting the significance that work holds for them and increased work opportunities (Fillenbaum & Maddox, 1974; Grad, 1977). Work after retirement can alleviate the stresses of retirement itself; therefore, it is clearly an area that deserves future research.

In summary, although part-time and full-time work after retirement appear applicable to only a small proportion of the older population, they represent two work/retirement patterns. With adequate data, the social stress model could be applied to these role shifts as well as to the more common pattern of complete cessation of employment.

Review Questions

1. *How is the experience of retirement affected by the type of work engaged in before retirement?*

2. *Some sociologists believe that* retired person *constitutes a meaningful social role; others do not. What do you think, and why?*

3. *The "proper" retirement age varies widely by occupation. It isn't unusual for a professional baseball player to retire in his early 40s or even his late 30s. For many college teachers, on the other hand, the established age for retirement is 65. In what ways might the age of retirement influence the process of adjustment to that role transition?*

4. *Under current Social Security regulations, unless a person is 72 or older, there is a limit as to how much money he or she can earn and still be eligible for retirement benefits. Given available evidence, if a policy of unlimited earnings was adopted (no matter how much a person age 65 or over earned, he or she would still receive full Social Security retirement benefits), in what way and to what extent might this influence participation of older people in the labor force?*

5. *In spite of the fact that most older workers are as productive as younger workers (and have lower absenteeism rates), many employers are reluctant to hire older workers (a phenomenon known as* age discrimination*). Similarly, in spite of the fact that mandatory retirement has been abolished for most occupations, many employers would prefer mandatory retirement at a fixed age or length of service. Can you determine some of the reasons for these employment practices and preferences?*

6

Role Transitions in Later Life: The World of the Family

Family life is a major area of adulthood. All of us are born into families, and during adulthood most of us establish families of our own. Family life is undoubtedly the context in which most people establish and participate in intimate and affective relationships. (Again we are reminded of Freud's dictum that the major psychosocial tasks of adulthood are to love and to work.)

Several role changes and role transitions associated with family life are commonly experienced during middle age and old age. Proceeding in usual chronological order, the first of these transitions involves the departure of the last child from the home—an event frequently referred to as the **empty nest.** This role transition has been hypothesized as having a major impact on the parental couple. Not only are day-to-day parental duties relinquished, but the couple also must negotiate changes in their relationship. Next, the status and role of grandparent are acquired, providing opportunities for new kinds of affective, family-based relationships between grandparents and grandchildren. In addition, relationships between grandparents and their own children often change as the latter acquire parental responsibilities. Widowhood is the most dramatic family-based role transition—one that poses a major adaptive challenge to the remaining spouse. Finally, remarriage is an increasingly common event among widowed and divorced older persons.

In this chapter, each of these transitions is examined. Our model of adjustment to social stress will be used, in conjunction with available research findings, to determine the degree to which and the conditions under which these role shifts are experienced as either debilitating or enriching. However, before we examine these role shifts, we will discuss the context of family life in middle age and old age.

The Context of Family Life in Middle Age and Old Age

In order to better understand the family-based role shifts that are common in middle age and old age, we need to examine the context of family life during late adulthood. Two issues are especially important here: (1) the nature and quality of the relationships between generations of family members, and (2) the nature and quality of marital relationships in middle age and old age. We will discuss these issues in the following paragraphs.

Generational Relationships

A variety of demographic factors, including life expectancy, the age of parents when their children are born, and the age at which children leave home, have resulted in many three-generation families in our society. (Indeed, four-generation families are increasingly common.) In industrialized societies, the **nuclear family** tends to be both the preferred and the actual pattern of family structure. During the early years of marriage, the average nuclear family consists of a young married couple and their children. During the later years of marriage, when offspring establish their own nuclear households, the parents comprise a couple-based nuclear household.

An **extended family** is one in which members of three or more generations of a family share a single household. Extended-family households are not typical in industrialized societies. For example, in the United States, only 15% of older women and 7% of older men live with their children or with other relatives (Hendricks & Hendricks, 1977). The results of a number of social surveys suggest that, in our society, both younger and older adults express a clear preference for separate households, even when this means that a widowed older parent must live alone (Sussman, 1976; Troll, 1971).

Traditionally, observers of the social aspects of aging assumed that nuclear households were detrimental to older persons, hypothesizing that such arrangements place older family members at risk for loneliness and social isolation. However, as Troll (1971) and Sussman (1976) note in reviews that focus on the family lives of older persons, this assumption appears to be unfounded. Most older persons maintain close, viable, and satisfying relationships with their adult children. Interaction among older and younger family members, including visits, letters, and telephone calls, tends to be frequent. In addition, most older and younger family members report satisfaction with the frequency and quality of intergenerational family relationships.

This pattern of frequent and satisfying interaction among generations of adult family members living in independent households has been referred to as a *modified extended family system* (Hill, 1970; Troll, 1971). Rosenmayr and Köckeis (1963) use the phrases "intimacy at a distance" and "revocable detachment" to describe common patterns of intergenerational attachment. *Intimacy at a distance* refers to the ability of family members to sustain meaningful relationships in the absence of frequent interaction. *Revocable detachment* refers to the fact that dormant emotional ties can be mobilized when they are needed or desired. These terms convey an essential message —most older people are able to maintain viable and satisfying relationships with younger family members, in spite of separate living arrangements.

Patterns of resource exchange or mutual aid among older and younger family members have been the subject of empirical inquiry. As noted previously, later life tends to be characterized by moderate amounts of resource loss. In spite of this, available evidence suggests that older persons aren't always the recipients of assistance from younger family members. Instead, all generations of family members participate in complex patterns of social resource exchange, and each generation receives *and* contributes assistance in times of need.

One study of family development among three generations— grandparents, parents, and young married children—suggested that: (1) the parental generation contributed the most assistance and held a patron-like status, (2) the grandparents received the most assistance and were viewed as dependent, and (3) the young married children provided and received moderate assistance and were viewed as reciprocators (Hill, 1970). Although we can't determine which generation gives or receives the most assistance, the important point is that older family members are involved in patterns of mutual aid and resource exchange with younger family members.

The preceding discussion refers to general patterns of family relationships. It doesn't imply that there are no older persons who are socially isolated or estranged from their families. Undoubtedly, some older persons are isolated from their families or are dissatisfied with their family relationships. Moreover, these general patterns differ somewhat, depending on a family's general socioeconomic status, the gender of the family members involved, and the family's race or ethnic-group membership. Available research suggests that patterns of interaction and mutual aid are somewhat more extensive among lower-class and working-class families than they are among middle-class families (Adams, 1968b; Aldous, 1967), that women participate in complex patterns of family interaction and exchange more often than men (Aldous, 1967; Berardo, 1967; Hagestad & Snow, 1977), and that Black and ethnic families develop more extensive patterns of intergenerational interaction and exchange (Hays & Mindel, 1973).

In summary, in our society, even though adult family members tend to live in separate households, they engage in complex and extensive patterns of interaction and social exchange. In addition, most older family members express a clear preference for independent living arrangements, and report that they are satisfied with the quantity and quality of intergenerational interaction.

Marital Relationships

Marital couples make up the core of the nuclear household. Although child-rearing requires a significant amount of a couple's life, the marital dyad forms a separate nuclear unit prior to the birth of the first child as well as after the departure of the last child from the parental home. Even while children are in the home, the marital couple is the functional core of the family unit. For most adults, then, the primary source of day-to-day family interaction, intimacy, and shared household responsibility is a marital partner; therefore, the nature and quality of the marital relationship is an important component of family life in middle age and old age.

Numerous studies suggest that marital satisfaction follows an identifiable and fairly dramatic course across the adult years. The general form of this pattern is a u-shaped curve. Levels of marital satisfaction are quite high during the early years of marriage (when most couples are in their 20s). They decrease somewhat for couples in their 30s, reach their lowest point in the 40s, and then increase through late middle age and peak again during old age (Burr, 1970; Campbell, Converse, & Rodgers, 1976; Rollins & Feldman, 1970). Therefore, it appears that middle age is characterized by relatively low levels of marital satisfaction, whereas the later years of marriage are usually quite satisfying.

A note of caution: the vast majority of studies that deal with the relationship between age and marital status are based on cross-sectional rather than longitudinal data. Therefore, the reported pattern could reflect age differences among historically unique cohorts rather than a characteristic of the marital life course. In addition, the use of cross-sectional data inherently favors intact, long-term marriages. Unhappy marriages are likely to end in divorce, and, in later life, a large proportion of highly dissatisfying marriages will have been terminated by divorce, leaving the happier, intact marriages to be sampled and studied. In spite of these methodological cautions, keep in mind that a relationship between age and marital satisfaction has been reported in a variety of studies, suggesting that the relationship is a real one.

If age-linked differences in marital satisfaction aren't purely a result of the use of cross-sectional data, it is important to identify the facets of middle life and later life that might explain this relationship. Several possible explanations have been proposed. First, "mid-life crisis" has been suggested as a cause of low levels of both marital satisfaction and general life satisfaction in middle life (Brim, 1976; Levinson, 1978). According to this perspective, middle age is a time during which individuals reassess the meaning and accomplishments of their lives, including their marital and familial relationships. It is a period of reappraisal that is usually somewhat painful, but it offers possibilities of renewal and subsequent increases in satisfaction. This perspective is most closely related to theories of developmental psychology, and, thus far, it has limited empirical support.

A second possible explanation is the fact that, over time, a kind of socialization takes place during which marital partners acquire and develop increasingly similar clusters of norms and values and evolve a shared view of the world that is conducive to marital satisfaction. Kerckhoff (1966) describes a "strain toward consistency" among older married couples. In this study, interviews with older couples indicated that value similarity between spouses is related to marital satisfaction. It should be noted that this study was based on cross-sectional data; therefore, it is unclear whether the value similarity between spouses developed over time or the individuals married persons with values that were similar to their own. The hypothesis that converging values increase marital satisfaction clearly merits further research.

Several authors note that reported decreases in marital satisfaction tend to coincide with increased child care responsibilities, whereas reported increases in marital satisfaction in late middle age tend to coincide with the age at which children typically leave the parental home (Burr, 1970; Rollins & Feldman, 1970). These facts suggest that child-rearing responsibilities take a toll on marital satisfaction. This line of reasoning is supported by two additional research findings. First, available evidence suggests that decreased levels of marital satisfaction reported in middle age are more characteristic of women than men (Burr, 1970; Campbell, Converse, & Rodgers, 1976; Rollins & Feldman, 1970). Since women have traditionally been more involved in child care than men, this difference could reflect the significance of child-rearing responsibilities for marital satisfaction. Second, married persons without children report significantly higher levels of marital satisfaction during middle adulthood than married persons with children (Campbell, Converse, & Rodgers, 1976).

The results of the studies cited here don't suggest that parents typically regret the child-rearing decision. Indeed, as Campbell, Converse, and Rodgers (1976) point out, in spite of the clear evidence that suggests a decline in marital satisfaction during the child-raising years (especially while children are in their teens) parents uniformly deny that they regret the decision to become parents or that they dislike the parental role. Apparently, either the parental role is valued in spite of the fact that it takes an emotional toll or parents don't attribute their midlife dissatisfactions to the responsibilities of child rearing.

In summary, marital relationships are a major component of family life throughout the adult years—a factor that is heightened by the nuclear family structure characteristic of modern, industrialized societies. Available evidence suggests that satisfaction with marital relationships tends to be relatively low during middle age but increases during later life. Several factors might be related to increased marital satisfaction in later years, the most convincing of which is the departure of children from the parental home.

The impact of children on marital satisfaction and social adjustment leads us to a consideration of the first role change of middle life—the departure of children from the parental home.

The Empty Nest

The *empty nest* refers to the departure of the last child from the parental home. Although families with more than one child deal with the departure of a child more than once, the departure of the last child is viewed as especially significant, because it marks the end of day-to-day child-rearing responsibilities and the return of the marital partners to a one-generation, couple-based household. Early discussions of this topic hypothesized that the departure of the last child from the home is a stressful event, particularly for mothers. Presumably, the departure of the last child disrupts customary behavior patterns, requires relinquishment of meaningful role duties that help to structure time, and involves loss of a major source of identity and emotional meaning for parents.

Available research provides little, if any, evidence to support the theory that parents typically perceive the departure of the last child from the home as stressful. The empty nest appears to be a low-impact event that has little positive or negative effect on parents' identities or levels of social adjustment. To the extent that the presence or absence of children *does* influence identity and adjustment, the empty nest appears to be a positive event that enhances the life quality of the parents. Indeed, the years immediately preceding the departure of children from the home are more likely to be viewed as stressful than either the transition stage itself or its long-term consequences.

Two types of evidence support this conclusion regarding the positive effects of the empty nest. First, as previously described, several cross-sectional surveys of marital satisfaction across adulthood suggest increased satisfaction after the departure of the last child (Burr, 1970; Campbell, Converse, & Rodgers, 1976; Rollins & Feldman, 1970). The Rollins and Feldman study provides a clear illustration of this pattern. (See Table 6-1, which presents the distributions of marital satisfaction for men and women at eight

TABLE 6-1. *Marital Satisfaction by Present Stage of the Family Life Cycle, Reported in Percentages.*

Stage of Family Life Cycle	Degree Satisfied					
	Husbands			Wives		
	Very	Quite	Less	Very	Quite	Less
Establishment (newly married)	55	39	6	74	22	4
New parents	69	23	8	76	18	6
Preschool children	61	31	8	50	33	17
School-age children	39	45	16	35	44	21
Adolescent children	44	41	15	17	38	15
Launching center	9	25	66	8	16	76
Postparental	24	13	63	17	13	70
Aging family	66	20	4	82	14	4

From "Marital Satisfaction Over the Family Life Cycle," by B. G. Rollins and H. Feldman, *Journal of Marriage and the Family*, 1970, *32*, 24. Copyright 1970 by the National Council on Family Relations. Reprinted by permission of the authors and publisher.

family stages.) In this study, marital satisfaction is related to family stage rather than age. The results clearly illustrate the effects of children on satisfaction with marital relationships. The lowest levels of marital satisfaction are reported by both men and women during the family stage referred to as the *launching stage*. In contrast, levels of marital satisfaction are high during the post-parental and aging family stages. Although this pattern reflects levels of satisfaction for both men and women, the levels are more pronounced for women.

The second line of evidence is provided by several studies that included interviews of or structured questionnaires administered to middle-aged parents. These studies specifically focused on perceptions and evaluations of postparental life (Deutscher, 1968; Hagestad, 1977; Hagestad & Snow, 1977; Harkins, 1978). In all of these studies, respondents reported that they were highly satisfied with postparental life and cited a variety of specific benefits that were a result of the departure of the last child from the home. These benefits included increased personal freedom, a sense of accomplishment resulting from the successful launching of their child to an independent lifestyle, and the experience of discovering the adult child as a social resource.

Although the empty nest has been referred to as stressful, it is not perceived as such by a majority of parents. This doesn't mean that the empty-nest transition is uniformly experienced as enhancing or even nonstressful. One of the advantages of the social stress perspective is that it cautions us to determine the conditions under which a given life event is and is not perceived as stressful. Although the empty-nest transition is not typically perceived as stressful, some individuals do find the transition a difficult one.

Women are apparently more affected than men by the departure of the last child. Evidence from social surveys suggests that the relationship between marital satisfaction and family life-cycle stage is stronger for women than men (Campbell, Converse, & Rodgers, 1976; Rollins & Feldman, 1970). Moreover, women are more concerned than men about the impending empty-nest transition (Lowenthal & Chiriboga, 1972), and they are more likely to perceive the postparental years as a time of increased freedom and to view their adult children as a new social resource (Hagestad, 1977; Hagestad & Snow, 1977).

Temporal issues also appear to influence adjustment to the empty-nest transition. For example, although Bourque and Back (1977) report that the empty nest is a relatively low-impact life event, the departure of the last child from the home tends to be perceived as a mildly positive event during the middle years and a slightly negative event when experienced at later ages. Similarly, Harkins (1978) reports that the timing of the empty-nest transition is important; with mothers of "off-track" children reporting lower levels of psychological well-being. Some evidence suggests that those individuals for whom parenting is a major source of personal identity are likely to experience a sense of loss as a result of the empty nest transition (Lowenthal & Chiriboga, 1972). Although the evidence is limited, at least a few of the variables that condition perceptions of stress have been identified.

The empty-nest syndrome illustrates several of the issues regarding social stress that were raised in previous chapters. First, research results regarding adjustment to the departure of the last child illustrate the importance of perceptions of stress. The presumed sense of stress accompanying the empty nest appears to be largely nonexistent. Second, the empty-nest transition may be a good illustration of the beneficial impact of anticipatory socialization. Of all the role changes and role transitions common in middle life and later life, the empty-nest transition is probably the most expected, the most normatively valued (given our society's clear preference for nuclear-family households), and, therefore, the most likely to be prepared for by means of anticipatory socialization. Moreover, the empty-nest transition is a low-impact event, because the parent/child relationship is altered rather than terminated.

Grandparenthood

Although grandparenthood is a common role transition in middle life and later life, social scientists have devoted little energy to the study of grandparenting and its significance for both grandparents and grandchildren. All of the available evidence is based primarily on three studies.

Neugarten and Weinstein (1964) examined the significance and style of grandparenting among 70 middle-class couples. They investigated the couples' feelings regarding the grandparent role, the meaning of the role, and the style of grandparenting—that is, the predominant theme of the grandparent/grandchild relationship. Table 6-2 summarizes the results of their study. First, although most grandmothers and grandfathers reported that they were comfortable with their roles as grandparents, a significant number of both grandmothers and grandfathers expressed some feelings of discomfort with the grandparent role.

The respondents in Neugarten and Weinstein's study differed in their perceptions of the role of grandparent. For some, grandchildren were viewed as a source of biological renewal or continuity. This view was the one most frequently reported among this sample. Other respondents reported that grandparenthood provided a satisfying family relationship that resulted in emotional

TABLE 6-2. *Comfort with Grandparent Role, Meaning of Role, and Style of Grandparenting among 70 Grandmothers and 70 Grandfathers, reported in percentages.*

	Grandmothers	Grandfathers
Comfort with Grandparent Role		
Comfortable, pleasant	59	61
Difficulty, discomfort	36	29
Insufficient data	5	10
Meaning of Grandparent Role		
Biological renewal or continuity	42	23
Emotional self-fulfillment	19	27
Resource person to grandchild	4	11
Vicarious achievement through grandchild	4	4
Remote; little effect on self	27	29
Insufficient data	4	6
Style of Grandparenting		
The formal	31	33
The fun-seeking	29	24
The parent surrogate	14	0
The reservoir of family wisdom	1	6
The distant figure	19	29
Insufficient data	6	8

From "The Changing American Grandparent," by B. L. Neugartein and K. K. Weinstein, *Journal of Marriage and the Family*, 1964, 26, 201. Copyright 1964 by the National Council on Family Relations. Reprinted by permission of the authors and publisher.

self-fulfillment. Some maintained a closer relationship with their grandchildren than they had achieved with their own children. A smaller proportion of the respondents indicated that grandparenthood offered them an opportunity to serve as a resource for their grandchildren or to experience a vicarious sense of achievement as a result of their grandchildren's accomplishments. Finally, some respondents reported that they felt relatively remote from their grandchildren and believed that grandparenthood had little effect on their identities or their lifestyles.

In their study, Neugarten and Weinstein also examined styles of grandparenting, or the way in which the grandparent role is enacted. Five grandparenting styles were identified: formal, fun seeking, parent surrogate, reservoir of family wisdom, and distant. The formal style involves a clear distinction between parenting and grandparenting. Although formal grandparents maintain an active interest in their grandchildren, behavioral involvement tends to be limited and formal. The fun-seeking style of grandparenthood is characterized by informality and shared leisure activities between grandparents and grandchildren. Grandparents who maintain a parent-surrogate style take on major child-rearing responsibilities. Neugarten and Weinstein point out that this grandparenting style appears to be restricted to grandmothers and is initiated by parents. A less common style of grandparenting is the reservoir of family wisdom style, in which grandparents are treated in a deferential manner and viewed as a major source of authority. Finally, the distant-grandparenting style involves interaction between grandparents and grandchildren that is fleeting, formal, and remote.

Neugarten and Weinstein describe both sex and age differences in styles of grandparenting. The parent-surrogate style is consistently used by grandmothers, whereas the reservoir of family wisdom style is predominantly used by grandfathers. Younger grandparents (age 65 and younger) are more likely to use the fun-seeking or distant grandparenting style, whereas older grandparents more frequently adopt a formal grandparenting style. Neugarten and Weinstein concluded that the variety of grandparenting styles suggests that the role of grandparent is a relatively informal one that permits individuals to develop relationships compatible with their personal preferences.

Robertson (1977) examined styles of grandparenting among 125 grandmothers. She developed a four-part typology of grandparenting style based on two dimensions. The first dimension consists of an individual's personal orientation toward grandparenting; the second dimension consists of an individual's perceptions of the social and normative meanings attached to grandparenthood. Figure 6-1 presents the four resulting grandparenting styles, along with the proportion of the sample engaged in each style.

Remote Grandmothers perceived few social and normative meanings in grandparenthood and reported low amounts of personal involvement in grandparenting. These grandmothers were intermediate in age and educational attainment (compared with the rest of the sample) and were typically widows

Personal Orientation

		Low	High
Social/Normative Orientation	Low	Remote 28%	Individualized 17%
	High	Symbolic 26%	Apportioned 29%

FIGURE 6-1 *Robertson's typology of grandparent role meaning. (From "Grandmotherhood: A Study of Role Conceptions," by J. F. Robertson,* Journal of Marriage and the Family, *1977, 38, 168. Copyright 1977 by the National Council on Family Relations. Reprinted by permission of the publisher.)*

who were not employed outside the home. The remote grandmothers scored lowest of all groups on life satisfaction and friendship patterns, but relatively high on community involvement. As would be expected, these grandmothers reported low levels of behavioral involvement with their grandchildren.

Individualized grandmothers attached little social and normative meaning to the grandparent role, but they attached personal significance to the role. These grandmothers were the oldest and had the lowest levels of educational attainment. They were typically widows who weren't employed outside the home. Socially, they exhibited high levels of friendship involvement, moderate levels of life satisfaction, and low levels of community involvement. These grandmothers reported frequent and satisfying interactions with their grandchildren.

Symbolic grandmothers attached significant amounts of normative and social meaning to the grandparent role, but they report little personal attachment to or behavioral involvement with their grandchildren. These women ranked highest in educational attainment, frequency of contact with friends, and life satisfaction. They ranked low in community involvement, and were usually married and employed outside the home. (This group was the youngest of the four groups of grandmothers.)

Apportioned grandmothers attached a significant amount of social and normative meaning to the grandparent role and were the most personally and behaviorally involved with their grandchildren. These women were typically widows who were not employed. They reported moderate levels of life satisfaction and contacts with friends. In addition, these grandmothers maintained relatively high levels of community involvement.

These profiles suggest that a variety of social and demographic characteristics are related to each grandparenting style.

Both the Neugarten and Weinstein (1964) and the Robertson (1977) studies suggest that a variety of grandparenting styles are preferred and practiced. These studies assume that the style of grandparenting is a characteristic of the grandparent rather than of the grandparent/grandchild interaction. Neither study addresses the issue of multiple grandparent/grandchild relationships. It is possible, for example, that grandparents exhibit different styles of grandparenting, depending on the particular grandchild in question. This is one of a number of important research questions concerning grandparenthood that merits further attention.

The significance of grandparents was examined by Robertson (1976) in a study of 86 young adult grandchildren, age 18 to 26. In general, these respondents reported very favorable attitudes toward their grandparents. Moreover, they indicated that, although they felt a sense of responsibility toward their grandparents, they didn't expect concrete rewards from them. These young adult grandchildren felt that their parents were instrumental in setting the style and intensity of grandparent/grandchild relationships.

These three studies indicate that grandparenting is an informal role that is free of normative guidelines. Grandparents and grandchildren apparently view the grandparent/grandchild relationship as an expressive rather than an instrumental one. In addition, both grandparents and grandchildren view the intermediate, parental generation as the most influential factor in defining the nature of the grandparent/grandchild relationship.

The role transition involved in becoming a grandparent fits our model of adjustment to social stress in only limited ways. One reason for this is that grandparenthood doesn't appear to be a high-impact life event. Normative guidelines are so few and so vague that individuals pursue the style of relationship they find most comfortable. Without clear patterns of relationships, it's difficult to apply data to the social stress model (or to *any* model). Moreover, grandparenthood is not a bounded event. Although becoming a grandparent is readily identifiable, relationships between grandparents and grandchildren are ongoing. As a result, the kind of "snapshot" view used in the social stress model cannot be applied to an examination of long-term grandparent/grandchild relationships.

Widowhood

Widowhood poses a major adaptive challenge to the remaining spouse. Although the death of a spouse can occur during any life stage, older couples are most frequently affected by this event. Table 6-3 presents rates of widowhood among individuals age 65 or older in 1975. As the table indicates, rates of widowhood are much higher among persons age 75 or older. Moreover, much larger proportions of older women are widowed, reflecting the fact that women typically live longer than men and tend to marry men somewhat older than themselves. Nearly 70% of women age 75 and older are widowed.

In one of the most detailed studies of widowhood available, Lopata (1973a) maintains that widowhood is a social role. The primary duties associ-

Marital Status	Men		Women	
	65–74	75+	65–74	75+
Single	4.3	5.5	5.8	5.8
Married (spouse present)	81.8	68.3	47.3	22.3
Divorced	3.1	1.2	3.3	1.5
Widowed	8.8	23.3	41.9	69.4

[a] Column totals are slightly less than 100%, reflecting missing data.

From *Current Population Reports,* Series P-20, No. 287, p. 8. U. S. Bureau of the Census. Washington, D. C. : U. S. Government Printing Office, 1975.

ated with this role are: (1) to learn to live independently, and (2) to successfully engage with society as a widowed person. On the other hand, some authors view widowhood as a major role *loss*—one that is stressful in part because the normative guidelines and role privileges of being a spouse are lost, and the widow is left with few viable substitutes.

We will now examine adjustment to widowhood from a social stress perspective. The social stress model will be used, along with available research findings, to examine the degree to which widowhood is stressful and to determine the factors that affect the adjustment process.

The Death of a Spouse As a Stressful Event

Available research consistently testifies that the death of a spouse is perceived as highly stressful and disruptive, regardless of the quality of the marital relationship or the circumstances of the spouse's death. The stressful aspects or components of widowhood that have been identified are discussed in the following paragraphs.

Grief, or bereavement, is the predominant stress of widowhood, particularly during the first few weeks or months after the spouse's death (Glick, Weiss, & Parkes, 1974; Lopata, 1969, 1973a; Marris, 1958; Parkes, 1972). Some authors believe that grief—a process of emotional pain and recovery—is characterized by a sequence of identifiable stages. Parkes (1972) describes grief as a progression of emotional states—numbness, pining and yearning, and depression—that is eventually overcome. Similarly, Glick and his associates (1974) state that the initial stages of grief are characterized by feelings of shock, disbelief, sadness, and lack of self-control. Intermediate stages of grief involve introspective mourning, a sense of the spouse's continued presence, and a compulsive search for meaning. Eventually, emotional upheaval becomes less severe and less frequent. Virtually all authors agree that the grief process varies greatly in intensity and duration from one individual to another.

Guilt and Anger are often experienced during the early stages of bereavement (Glick et al., 1974; Parkes, 1972). Some spouses feel guilty about the way they treated their partners. Others experience anger, because they are left to cope with practical problems and emotional pain. Although guilt and anger are not universal components of the grief process, they are commonly experienced during bereavement.

Loneliness is a long-term consequence of the death of a spouse. Both Lopata (1969, 1973a) and Glick and his associates (1974) report that persons who have been widowed for an extended period of time continue to report feelings of loneliness. Lopata (1969) points out that loneliness is a result of a variety of losses. In her study of 300 widows, respondents reported that they missed eight components of the marital relationship: the husband as (1) a unique individual with special qualities, (2) someone to love, (3) a source of being loved, (4) a companion, (5) someone to help structure and organize time, (6) a partner in the division of household labor, (7) a source of social status, and (8) a source of lifestyle. Several authors also note that disruptions of friendships, especially couple-based friendships, contribute to feelings of loneliness during widowhood (Blau, 1961; Glick et al., 1974; Lopata, 1969, 1973a).

All of these components reflect the emotional stresses and losses associated with the death of one's spouse. As Lopata notes, these emotional stresses are accompanied by very real material and structural losses (such as the loss of an income) and disruptions of established behavior patterns. All of these factors contribute to the perceptions of stress that typically accompany widowhood.

The Impact of Widowhood on Adjustment and Identity

Since overwhelming evidence indicates that the death of a spouse generates significant amounts of grief and loneliness, it isn't surprising that problems in adjustment and identity are usually components of widowhood. Although available evidence suggests that the vast majority of widowed persons eventually attain acceptable levels of adjustment and self-identity, widowhood typically involves at least short-term threats to identity and adjustment.

Adjustment. As I noted earlier, social adjustment has two components: (1) the ability to meet environmental demands, and (2) a sense of personal well-being. Research findings suggest that widowhood has a negative impact on these components of social adjustment.

Several authors suggest that widowhood frequently causes illness or deterioration in health. A variety of psychophysiological symptoms commonly accompany the grief process, the most common of which are loss of sleep and appetite (Glick et al., 1974; Marris, 1958; Parkes, 1972). These symptoms often persist for weeks or months and disrupt normal life routines. Moreover, at least one study suggests that negative health outcomes consequent to widowhood are more serious than isolated grief-related symptoms. Maddison and Viola (1968) reported that widowed persons showed significantly greater rates of health deterioration 13 months after a spouse's death than a group of married control subjects. The reasons for health decline remain uncertain. In part, increases in illness reflect the strains of the grief process. In addition, in many cases, the widowed spouse has spent a considerable period of time nursing a dying loved one—a task that can be physically and emotionally taxing.

Widowhood also takes a significant toll on one's sense of personal well-being. Numerous studies report that widowed persons consistently exhibit lower levels of life satisfaction and morale than married persons of the same age (Campbell, Converse, & Rodgers, 1976; Morgan, 1976). Widowed persons also exhibit higher rates of mental illness than individuals of comparable age who are married or have never been married, although divorced and separated persons display even higher rates of mental illness than widowed individuals (Warheit, et al., 1976).

Identity. Widowhood typically results in necessary identity changes. Usually, the role of husband or wife is a very important and pervasive aspect of one's identity. Following a spouse's death, this aspect of identity is no longer available, and an identity as a widowed person must be negotiated (Glick, et al., 1974; Lopata, 1973a). Adopting the identity of a widowed person can be difficult. For example, one of the frequently reported problems deals with sexual identity. Issues such as whether to date, when to start dating, and the desirability of remarriage are all a part of the task of renegotiating sexual identity. Many other spheres of life require similar negotiations.

In summary, a significant amount of research indicates that widowhood is typically a highly stressful life event. It is perceived as stressful—a perception that reflects the grief and loneliness that most widowed persons experience. Empirical research suggests that widowhood has a negative impact on both adjustment and identity.

Conditioning Variables: Factors That Affect Adjustment to Widowhood

Available evidence suggests that, eventually, most widowed persons successfully negotiate identity reformulations and attain acceptable and even satisfying levels of adjustment. However, in the short run, widowhood generates stress that affects identity and adjustment. In this context, conditioning variables are those factors that facilitate or impede the process of adjustment to widowhood. Researchers have identified four types of variables that affect the complex process of adjustment to widowhood: social status variables, personal resources, coping skills, and anticipatory socialization. These variables are discussed in the following paragraphs.

Social Status Variables. Social status variables are important indicators of an individual's position in the social structure and are pervasive factors in our life experience. Three social status variables have been related to the complex process of adjustment to widowhood: gender, age at widowhood, and race or ethnic-group membership.

Gender. Although several studies report significant sex differences in adjustment to widowhood, the patterns of their results are complex and do not indicate that either gender is clearly at an advantage. Several studies report that men find widowhood more difficult in terms of health, personal well-being, and general adjustment (Adams, 1968b; Berardo, 1970; Glick, et al., 1974). However, other studies suggest that men fare better than women, citing evidence that men typically have higher incomes, participate more in friendship networks and voluntary organizations (Atchley, 1975), complete the grief process more quickly than women (Glick, et al., 1974), and are more likely to remarry (Cleveland & Gianturco, 1976; Treas & Van Helst, 1976). Therefore, although several factors related to adjustment to widowhood are related to gender, it doesn't appear that these differences comprise a clear gender-related advantage.

Age at widowhood. The experiences of younger and older widowed persons differ significantly; however, it's impossible to conclude that one group fares better than the other. Younger widowed persons typically exhibit lower levels of personal well-being during widowhood but are much more likely to remarry than older widowed persons (Cleveland & Gianturco, 1976; Glick, et al., 1974). Conversely, older widowed persons display higher levels of life satisfaction and are much less likely to either remarry or express the desire to remarry (Heyman & Gianturco, 1973; Lopata, 1973a). Apparently, the identity reformulations negotiated during widowhood differ significantly, depending on the age at which widowhood occurs. Younger widowed persons are more likely to reactivate the role and identity of spouse, whereas older widowed individuals often view widowhood as the end of their identity as a marital partner.

Race or Ethnic-Group Membership. Nonwhites and persons in close-knit ethnic communities appear to adjust to widowhood with fewer problems than other people. Lopata (1973a) reported that nonwhite and ethnic widows adjust to widowhood more quickly and with less personal disorganization and change in life-style. Similarly, Morgan (1976) found levels of morale to be significantly lower among White widows than among White married women of comparable age, whereas there were no significant differences in morale among widows and married women who were Black or Mexican-American. These authors suggest that subcultural differences in normative structure (that is, the degree to which widowhood is an identifiable and structured role), orientations toward marriage, and social support account for these racial and ethnic patterns. They maintain that racial and ethnic subcultures are often characterized by structured guidelines for appropriate behavior during widowhood, less of a couple orientation between marital partners, and extensive informal social support systems.

Personal Resources. As I noted earlier, appropriate levels of relevant personal resources can help to lessen the impact of social stress and facilitate successful adjustment. Three types of personal resources have been related to adjustment to widowhood: income, social support, and education.

Income. Adequate financial assets facilitate adjustment to widowhood, whereas a lack of financial resources exacerbates the problems associated with widowhood. Atchley (1975) found that sufficient income is the strongest correlate of adjustment to widowhood. Similarly, Morgan (1976) found that differences in morale between widows and married women disappeared when the effects of income were statistically controlled. From a somewhat different perspective, one-fifth of a sample of 300 older widows reported that financial difficulties were a major problem of widowhood and one-fourth reported that inability to handle finances was a serious problem (Lopata, 1973a).

Social Support. The death of a spouse is a highly visible life event that mobilizes social support networks. Most widowed persons receive both specific task-oriented assistance and general emotional support from relatives and close friends. Widowed persons turn to relatives, especially their children, for support more frequently than they turn to their friends (Glick, et al., 1974; Lopata, 1973a; Marris, 1958). Moreover, widowed persons typically report frequent and close interactions with their own families, but they experience a decrease in contact with their in-laws (Glick, et al., 1974; Lopata, 1973a; Marris, 1958). According to several studies, friends provide a variety of services and are very helpful in the first few weeks of widowhood, but relationships with couple-based friends often become strained following the initial stages of widowhood (Glick, et al., 1974; Lopata, 1973a).

In spite of the very real assistance provided by friends and relatives, widowed persons appear to feel somewhat ambivalent about the social support they receive and the amount they are willing to accept. Although assistance is readily accepted at first, most widowed persons quickly develop a desire to be independent (Glick, et al., 1974; Marris, 1958). In addition, many widowed persons report that friends and relatives encouraged them to stop grieving sooner than they were able to (Marris, 1958). In spite of the very real nature of their support, frequent interaction with friends does not and apparently cannot lessen the grief and loneliness associated with widowhood (Glick, et al., 1974; Lopata, 1973a).

Nonetheless, social support networks usually continue to provide resources following the initial stages of widowhood. Adams (1968a) reported that, compared to the adult children of intact parental couples, the adult children of widows contribute greater amounts of assistance to and spend more time with their mothers. Usually, this assistance is offered willingly, although some adult children experience resentment if they must continue to provide support over a long period of time without receiving reciprocal support.

Education. High levels of education are conducive to smooth adjustment to widowhood (Lopata, 1973a, 1973b). Lopata reports that widows with higher levels of education are more likely to participate in community organizations and develop new friendships. In short, education appears to facilitate reengagement with society.

Coping Skills. The ability to cope is determined by personality characteristics that are conducive to effective problem-solving and by specific behavioral coping strategies.

Personality and Attitudinal Factors. Lopata (1973a) maintains that active, multidimensional problem-solving individuals are better able to cope with change, including the changes associated with widowhood. She believes that widowed individuals face major challenges of adjustment—renewed engagement with society and reorganization of identity and lifestyle. A self-initiating personality facilitates that engagement and reorganization.

Specific Coping Strategies. The evidence regarding specific coping strategies used to counter the stresses of widowhood is limited. The most frequently employed strategies resemble a list of time-honored, common-sense remedies. The therapeutic value of "keeping busy" is perhaps the most strongly endorsed coping strategy reported by widowed persons (Glick, et al., 1974). Along with this rather active approach, the more passive notion that "time heals all wounds" is a highly endorsed recommendation for working through the grief of widowhood (Glick, et al., 1974; Marris, 1958). In addition, a sizable proportion of widows seek medical assistance in dealing with the stresses of widowhood (Glick, et al., 1974). It's been reported that the use of psychotropic drugs and alcohol is beneficial during the initial stages of widowhood. In later stages of widowhood, however, the use of such substances often signals significant maladjustment.

Socializing Experiences

Anticipatory Socialization. Perhaps no variable that affects adjustment to widowhood has been examined as frequently as anticipatory socialization. Theoretically, if anticipatory socialization helps to minimize the stress of widowhood, empirical data should support two hypotheses. First, differences in adjustment to widowhood should be affected by the length of a spouse's illness or the degree to which a spouse's death was expected. If a spouse suffered from a chronic illness or had experienced multiple attacks before dying, the widowed spouse would presumably have time to mentally rehearse for widowhood and to go through a process of anticipatory grief. In the case of sudden, unexpected death, on the other hand, anticipatory socialization would be precluded. Second, persons who become widowed in later life would be expected to adjust more easily than persons who lose their spouses at relatively early ages. Since widowhood is most commonly experienced in later life, persons who are widowed in early or middle adulthood are less likely to have benefitted from anticipatory socialization. These hypotheses have been tested to some extent, but the results are somewhat ambiguous. Age differences in adjustment to widowhood were described previously.

Most studies that examine the impact of widowhood following deaths caused by acute versus chronic conditions report no significant differences in terms of the amount or nature of the grief experienced by the surviving spouse (Bornstein, Clayton, Halikas, Maurice, & Robins, 1973; Clayton, Halikas, Maurice, & Robins, 1973; Glick, et al., 1974) or the effects on his or her health (Gerber, Rusalem, Hannon, Battin, & Arkin, 1975). In spite of this general pattern, at least one study concludes that the grief process is more intense and generates more personal disorganization when a spouse's death is unexpected (Schwab, Chalmers, Conroy, Farris, & Markush, 1975). Furthermore, Glick and his associates (1974) suggest that the degree to which a spouse's death is expected has some rather subtle effects on adjustment to widowhood. In spite of the fact that an expected death doesn't diminish the amount of grief experienced, they found that the process of grief is more quickly completed, the specific coping strategies used are more effective, and the long-term level of adjustment is higher among widowed persons who expected their spouses' deaths.

The Quality of the Marital Relationship. Although widowhood is characterized by intense grief and emotional upheaval regardless of the quality of a marital relationship, a surviving spouse's adjustment and identity changes are related to the nature and quality of the marital relationship he or she has lost. The degree of couple orientation—the degree to which leisure activities, friendship networks, and division of household tasks are shared—appears to be an important issue in this regard. Adjustment and identity changes consequent to widowhood are most dramatic and difficult in cases in which there was a strong couple orientation (Lopata, 1973a). In such situations, an individual's identity as a partner in an intense, mutual relationship is necessarily altered. On the other hand, spouses who survive marriages that were characterized by separate activities, friends, and household duties experience less disruption of established behavior patterns and sources of identity in widowhood. As Lopata points out, marriages with a high degree of couple orientation are common among middle-class persons, whereas lower-class couples frequently adhere to a doctrine of separate domains for spouses. In a sense, then, the nature and quality of a marital relationship serves as a socialization experience that either prepares individuals for an independent lifestyle during widowhood or makes adoption of an independent lifestyle very difficult.

The Process of Adjustment to Widowhood

It's important to acknowledge the temporal patterns of adjustment to widowhood. Recovery from initial grief is itself a process, and the entire sequence of adjustment to widowhood is a longer and more complex process. Most available studies of widowhood involve cross-sectional research designs and, therefore, are less than optimal for tracing the process of adjustment. Although cross-sectional studies permit comparisons of persons who have been widowed for varying lengths of time, longitudinal studies are the preferred design for observing changes over a period of time.

The most comprehensive longitudinal study of widowhood was conducted by Glick and his associates (1974). In this study, 85 widows and widowers, age 45 and younger, were interviewed three weeks, eight weeks, and 13 months after the death of their spouses. Four years after the death of their spouses, 68 of the respondents were interviewed again.

Glick and his associates describe a general pattern of adjustment to widowhood. The first six to eight weeks of widowhood are characterized by intense grief. Approximately eight weeks after the death of a spouse, a more lengthy, but less public period of grieving begins. By the end of the first year of widowhood, grieving becomes much less intense and the widowed individual moves tentatively toward developing an altered but stable lifestyle. At this point, long-term patterns of adjustment are identifiable. Two to four years after a spouse's death, the altered identity and lifestyle of the surviving spouse are usually solidified. There are, of course, individual variations of this process, but this is the typical pattern.

Since the sample in Glick's study was relatively young, caution should be exercised in generalizing these results to older widowed persons. In spite of this, the process of adjustment described by Glick and his associates is compatible with the findings of cross-sectional studies of older widows (Lopata, 1973a).

Typologies of Adjustment to Widowhood

Two studies propose typologies of patterns of adjustment to widowhood. Since the two studies are based on very different samples, the following comparison of these typologies should be especially useful.

Glick and his associates examined widowhood among middle-aged and younger adults. After longitudinal observations, the authors proposed a typology of five patterns of adjustment—four successful lifestyles and one unsuccessful pattern. Table 6-4 illustrates the five patterns of adjustment and the percentages of widows and widowers who exhibited these patterns. The first and predominant pattern of adjustment was remarriage. According to Glick, et al., individuals who chose this pattern were able to work through their grief for their former spouse and establish meaningful and satisfying re-marriages. Two other successful patterns (less frequently exhibited) involved the organization of an individual's life around either an intimate relationship that didn't lead to remarriage or relationships with relatives (usually children). A fourth successful pattern (exhibited almost as frequently as remarriage) was the development of a satisfying lifestyle independent of close relationships with other people. Finally, a small proportion of the sample failed to adjust to widowhood. They exhibited chaotic, unstable lifestyles.

Based on indepth interviews with 300 widows age 50 to 85 who had been widowed for varying lengths of time, Lopata (1973a) described three types of widows: the modern widow, the traditional widow, and the social isolate. Modern widows report a period of intense grief and moderate personal disorganization following the death of their husbands. Over a period of time, however, they were able to negotiate relevant identity changes, establish satisfying, independent lifestyles, and become involved in society again. For the traditional widows, widowhood had little impact on either identity or lifestyle. These women pursue the activities and interests they pursued before they were widowed. Apparently, these women's marriages were characterized by separate activities, and widowhood necessitates little change in their routines. This successful pattern of adjustment is most commonly found among women in ethnic or racial subcultures, where normative support for this style of widowhood exists. Finally, social isolates display a less success-ful style of adjustment. They are unable to engage with society in a construc-

TABLE 6-4. *Typology of Adjustment to Widowhood, by Sex, Reported in Percentages.*

Pattern of Adjustment	Widowers	Widows
Movement toward remarriage	50.0	29.8
Intimate relationship, no remarriage	0.0	10.6
Organize life around children or other relatives	16.7	10.6
Independent lifestyle	27.8	36.2
Disorganized, chaotic lifestyle	5.5	2.8

From Ira O. Glick, Robert S. Weiss, and C. Murray Parkes, *The First Year of Bereavement*. New York: John Wiley & Sons, 1974.

tive or personally satisfying manner. These women typically are of lower socioeconomic status, have attained low levels of education, and lack social support networks. They lack important resources that could facilitate the process of adjustment to widowhood.

Lopata doesn't provide distributions of the three patterns of adjustment to widowhood; therefore, distributions of successful and unsuccessful adaptation cannot be compared across the two studies. Nonetheless, the *patterns of adjustment* to widowhood described in the two studies can be compared. The most obvious difference between the two typologies is the prominence of remarriage or involvement in intimate, heterosexual relationships for younger widows and widowers. Older widows typically do not remarry; this is reflected in the styles of widowhood described by Lopata. The similarities between the two studies may be even more important than their differences. Both studies suggest that the vast majority of widowed persons ultimately exhibit acceptable adjustment and personal well-being and that there are *multiple* patterns of successful adjustment.

Using the Social Stress Model

In order to assess the usefulness of the social stress model in understanding adjustment to widowhood, we need to place the variables and characteristics discussed in the social stress model. Figure 6-2 presents the social stress model as a model of adjustment to widowhood.

The social stress model can be used as a framework for understanding the complexities as well as the general process of adjustment to widowhood. The model helps us to understand why widowhood is stressful and how it affects identity and adjustment. Moreover, it helps us to determine the factors that facilitate eventual adjustment to widowhood.

The social stress model also helps us to identify the areas and issues that are in need of additional research. The effects of several conditioning variables—especially social support and anticipatory socialization—remain ambiguous and require clarification. The entire topic of coping has been relatively neglected and merits further attention. Finally, more attention should be devoted to the temporal aspects of adjustment to widowhood. In spite of the need for further inquiry, the social stress model can be used as a framework for understanding adjustment to widowhood.

Remarriage: A Neglected Role Transition

Widowhood is *not* an irreversible status. Substantial numbers of widowed persons, as well as many divorced individuals, embark on second or even third marriages in middle life or later life. In 1970, although only 1% of

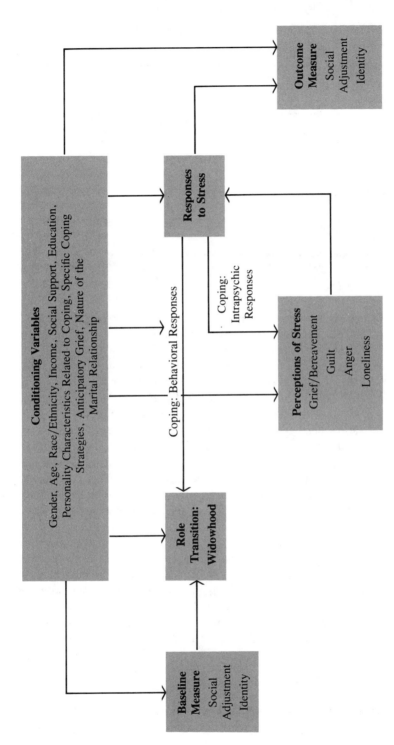

FIGURE 6-2 Adjustment to widowhood: A social stress model.

TABLE 6-5. *Probability That a New Widow or Widower Will Remarry (by Sex, Race, and Age)*.

Age	Widows		Widowers	
	White	Black	White	Black
20–24	.88	.51	.98	.84
25–34	.86	.25	.88	.70
35–44	.41	.23	.88	.43
45–54	.26	.07	.59	.25
55–64	.05	.06	.48	.21
65–74	.004	[a]	.24	.10
75 +	[a]	[a]	.06	[a]

[a]Probability is essentially zero.

Adapted from "Remarriage Probability After Widowhood: A Retrospective Method," by W. P. Cleveland and D. T. Gianturco, *Journal of Gerontology*, 1976, *31*(1), 100. Reprinted by permission.

all brides and 2% of all grooms were age 65 or older, this represents approximately 60,000 older people—the vast majority of whom have been previously married (Treas & Van Helst, 1976). Therefore, on the basis of sheer numbers alone, remarriage appears to be a role transition worthy of scientific attention. In spite of this, very little is known about remarriage in later life.

Much of the limited evidence currently available addresses demographic correlates of the likelihood of remarriage. Rates of remarriage differ widely for various demographically defined subgroups of the population. Four factors are strongly related to the likelihood of remarriage: previous marital status, age, gender, and race. Persons whose former marriages ended in divorce are more likely to remarry than widowed persons. This pattern holds true at all ages and for both men and women (Treas & Van Helst, 1976). Table 6-5 presents the probabilities of remarriage for new widows and widowers, taking into account the individual's age and race. This table permits us to simultaneously examine the effects of age, gender, and race on the probability of remarriage. As the table indicates, younger persons are more likely to remarry after widowhood than older persons, and widowers are more likely to remarry than widows. Less than 20% of all men widowed at age 65 or older remarry (which is a small percentage), but less than 5% of the women widowed at age 55 or older remarry. Finally, at all ages and for both sexes, Whites are more likely than Blacks to remarry after the death of a spouse.

The Desire to Remarry

There appear to be significant age differences in the desire to remarry as well as in the actual rates of remarriage. Glick and his associates (1974) report that, during the initial stages of widowhood, both widows and widowers typically express little interest in dating or establishing new relationships. In spite of this, two to four years after a spouse's death, 50% of the widowers and 29.8% of the widows in Glick et al.'s study had remarried. None of these persons reported any difficulty in finding a compatible mate or in establishing a satisfying relationship. Respondents in this study were age 45 or younger when they were widowed.

In contrast, Lopata (1973a) interviewed 300 widows age 50 to 86. Although none of these widows had remarried, almost 25% of them had been widowed more than once. The subjects of this study had been widowed from 1 to 20 or more years. Less than 20% of them expressed a desire to remarry —and those were typically the younger widows whose previous marriages had been characterized by a strong couple orientation. The reasons given for the desire to remain unmarried included the feeling that no other marriage could be as rewarding as the former marriage, the enjoyment of independence and freedom from responsibilities, the belief that another marriage wouldn't suit current lifestyles, and the desire to avoid nursing another spouse through an extended, fatal illness.

Adjustment to Remarriage in Later Life

Research that focuses on the process of adjustment to remarriage during later life is very limited. McKain's (1969) study of 100 couples who remarried during late adulthood is perhaps the most comprehensive study available. Respondents in this study reported that they chose to remarry because they wanted companionship and they wanted to avoid becoming dependent on their children. The desire for companionship was overwhelmingly the more frequent reason reported. No mention was made of romantic love. McKain was impressed by the fact that, in many cases, the new spouse was very similar to the previous spouse with regard to interests and background. These findings have been replicated in a more recent study (Vinick, 1978).

McKain noted six characteristics of successful remarriages. First, the most successful remarriages were between persons who had known each other a long time—a pattern that applies to first marriages as well. Second, the marital partners shared similar interests. Third, they appeared to have been well-adjusted prior to their remarriage. Fourth, they had adequate financial assets. Fifth, they had the approval of their children and friends. Finally, both spouses gave top priority to each other, rather than to their children.

The topic of adjustment to remarriage clearly merits further research. In theory, the social stress model should provide a useful framework for tracing the process of adjustment, accounting for different outcomes, and acknowledging and specifying the complexities of remarriage. Verification of the model's usefulness, however, must await the collection and analysis of additional empirical data.

Summary

Application of the social stress model to family-based role transitions common in later life has proved valuable. The model provides a useful framework for understanding both the general patterns and the complexities of adjustment to widowhood. The study of remarriage in middle life and later life might also be enhanced by the social stress perspective, although demonstration of this suggestion awaits additional empirical data.

This chapter sheds some light on the limitations as well as the benefits of the social stress model. Neither the empty-nest transition nor grandparenthood proved to be highly compatible with or clarified by use of the social stress model. In the case of the empty-nest transition, the crucial factor appears to be that the transition is usually a low-impact event. In the case of grandparenting, the fact that grandparenthood is not a bounded event posed problems. Apparently, the social stress model is less useful in dealing with ongoing or low-impact events than it is in dealing with bounded and high-impact role transitions.

The material presented in this chapter should help to clarify the conditions under which various family-based role transitions are and are not stressful and the conditions under which the social stress model is a useful conceptual framework.

Review Questions

1. *Zena Smith Blau (1961) demonstrated that the first person widowed in an established social group experiences more difficulty in adjusting to widowhood than persons widowed thereafter. What sociological principles can help to explain this pattern?*

2. *Harkins (1978) and Bourque and Back (1977) report that the empty-nest transition is more difficult if it occurs earlier or later than is typically the case. What sociological principles can help to explain this?*

3. *Robertson (1977) and Neugarten and Weinstein (1964) developed typologies to describe various kinds of relationships between grandparents and grandchildren. To what extent might these typologies apply to relationships between great grandparents and great grandchildren?*

4. *Why do some sociologists refer to the typical family form in our society as a modified extended-family system? What are the essential characteristics of such a system?*

5. *It has been suggested that lower levels of marital satisfaction and general life satisfaction in middle age reflect the impact of adolescent children in the family home. In what ways might the relationships between middle-aged persons and their older parents contribute to decreased feelings of well-being during middle age?*

7

Role Transitions in Later Life: Residential Relocation

Modern societies are mobile societies. For example, in the United States, nearly one-fifth of the population moves every year (U. S. Bureau of the Census, 1976). Although younger people move more frequently than older people, large numbers of people *do* relocate during middle life and later life. Reasons for relocation vary across the life cycle. Younger people usually relocate to pursue careers, purchase personal property, or expand family size. During middle and later years, relocation is more likely to reflect decreased family size (as a result of the empty-nest transition or the loss of a spouse), reductions in financial assets, the desire to live in a different climate or enter housing specifically designed for older people, or the need to live in an environment in which medical care and other services are provided.

At any life stage, residential relocation presents a significant adaptive challenge: the entire fabric of the physical and social environment is altered, requiring adjustment and the development of new life routines. In this chapter, two major types of residential relocation will be examined: **community-based moves** and **institutional relocation.** First, we will examine relocations that take place within the community. These range from moves from one dwelling unit to another to migration to different communities or geographical regions. When making this type of relocation, the individual maintains an independent community-based lifestyle. Next, we will examine relocations from the community to a residential institution or from one institution to another. The common factor in the process of institutional relocation is that the individual is no longer able to live independently in the community and must seek an environment in which services are provided. The social stress perspective, in conjunction with available research findings, will guide our examination of the impact of residential relocation on social adjustment in later life.

Community-Based Moves

Table 7-1 provides estimates of the percentages of U. S. residents (by age) who move over intervals of one and five years (U. S. Bureau of the Census, 1976). As the table indicates, older adults are less mobile than young adults. Nonetheless, in 1976 more than 25% of all Americans age 45 and older had changed residences within five years. Of this group, slightly more than half changed residences but remained in the same metropolitan area; the others participated in more distant moves. Residential relocation, then, is a relatively common transition in middle life and later life.

Is Residential Relocation Stressful?

Common sense dictates that one's home is a very special place—an emotionally sustaining place where one can be comfortable and at ease. A variety of common adages testify to the broadly held belief that one's home plays a significant role in personal well-being ("there's no place like home," and so on). Similarly, from a social science perspective, the residential environment is viewed as important for personal well-being because it represents a predictable and emotionally significant setting.

Change in residence is viewed as potentially stressful, because familiar life routines are disrupted, meaningful social relationships are altered, and emotional attachments are severed or strained. In addition to the disruption of established behavior patterns and the sense of personal loss that are results of residential relocation, two other factors influence the degree to which relocation is perceived as stressful: the distance involved in the move and the reason for the move.

Distance. An individual's place of residence is much more than a particular dwelling unit. Although the most immediate aspect of a residential environment is the housing unit itself, the dwelling unit is embedded in a larger and more complex environment that includes a neighborhood, a community, and a geographical region. Within this physical environment, friend-

TABLE 7-1. *Percentage of United States Population Residentially Mobile, at One Year and Five Year Intervals.*

Age	One Year	Five Years
1–4	28.8	NA[a]
5–14	17.4	49.6
15–19	18.1	44.5
20–24	44.4	75.4
25–34	29.4	71.6
35–44	15.6	45.2
45–54	10.7	32.4
55–64	9.0	27.8
65 and older	8.4	28.1
TOTAL, all ages	19.2	47.0

[a]Not Applicable

From *The Geographical Mobility of Americans: An International Comparison*, Series P-23, No. 64. U. S. Bureau of the Census. Washington, D. C.: U. S. Government Printing Office, 1976.

ships, social contacts, and other interpersonal relationships depend heavily on proximity and a stable environmental context. Therefore, distant moves create a great degree of disruption of established life routines and are likely to be experienced as stressful.

Reason for Relocation.   The reason for a move influences the degree to which the move is perceived as stressful. An individual who moves to a newer, larger, more convenient home will certainly perceive residential relocation differently than an individual who moves to a smaller apartment in order to survive financially. Similarly, a retired individual who moves to Florida in order to pursue a lifestyle of active leisure undoubtedly perceives relocation much differently than the retired person who moves to Arizona in order to retard further deterioration in health. Perhaps the most important issue here is whether the residential relocation is voluntary or involuntary. Although a voluntary relocation can disrupt established behavior patterns and generate some sense of loss, the fact that the move is desired is likely to lessen perceptions of stress. Involuntary relocations, on the other hand, are more likely to be perceived as stressful.

The Impact of Residential Relocation on Adjustment and Identity

Most available studies of the impact of residential relocation on adjustment and identity compare older people who move with older people who don't move. These studies view differences between the two groups as effects of residential relocation. Although this comparison is useful in identifying the effects of residential relocation on personal adjustment and identity, there are at least two additional important issues. First, the two groups actually might not be comparable; therefore, differences in adjustments and identity could reflect characteristics of the two groups rather than the effects of relocation. Second, although there are few studies that actually measure changes over time, it is important that adjustment to residential relocation be studied as a process. The long-term consequences of relocation on personal adjustment might differ from the short-term effects.

Social Adjustment. As I noted previously, social adjustment consists of the ability to meet environmental demands successfully and to maintain a sense of personal well-being. Researchers have studied the effects of residential relocation on both components of social adjustment.

Since health has an important influence on an individual's ability to successfully meet environmental demands, it's important to identify the effects of residential relocation on health. Five studies compared changes in health among older individuals who had relocated to health changes among similar older individuals who hadn't experienced residential relocation. Two studies reported better health among those who moved (Carp, 1966, 1977; Lipman, 1968), two studies reported better health among the nonmovers (Brand & Smith, 1974; Lawton & Cohen, 1974), and one study reported no significant difference in health between movers and nonmovers (Storandt & Wittels, 1975; Storandt, Wittels, & Botwinick, 1975).

Three studies have compared mortality rates among older people who relocate and those who do not. Again, the results are inconclusive. Carp (1977) reports lower mortality rates among the movers, whereas the other two studies report no differences among movers and nonmovers (Lawton & Yaffe, 1970; Wittels & Botwinick, 1974). At any rate, there is no evidence to suggest that community-based relocation results in increased mortality among the elderly.

Several authors have examined the impact of residential relocation on life satisfaction, morale, and other indicators of personal well-being. Again, the results of these examinations are inconclusive and do not permit straightforward generalization. Two studies report that life satisfaction is lower among movers than nonmovers (Brand & Smith, 1974; Kasteler, Gray, & Carruth, 1968), four studies found levels of personal adjustment to be higher among movers than nonmovers (Brody, Kleban, & Liebowitz, 1975; Carp, 1966, 1975a, 1975b; Lawton & Cohen, 1974; Lipman, 1968), and one study reported no significant differences in personal well-being between movers and nonmovers (Storandt & Wittels, 1975; Storandt, Wittels, & Botwinick, 1975).

Identity. Although residential relocation might be expected to influence identity, or a sense of self, few authors have examined this issue empirically. Carp (1966, 1977) and Storandt and her colleagues (Storandt & Wittels, 1975; Storandt, Wittels, & Botwinick, 1975) reported stable patterns of identity among older persons who experienced a change in residence.

In summary, it's difficult to determine the effects of residential relocation on social adjustment and identity in later life. Available research findings are inconclusive, and they preclude generalization. Since we can assume that the findings of these researchers don't merely reflect differences in the ways in which their studies were designed and conducted, we can assume that people react and adapt to residential relocation in very different ways. Some people appear to improve their lifestyles and levels of adjustment after residential relocation, whereas others experience some degree of negative outcome. In order to clarify these contradictions and ambiguities, it is crucial that we identify those factors that condition or mediate the relationship between residential relocation and social adjustment in later life. As we will see, by specifying these conditioning variables, we can partially resolve the inconsistencies in these research findings.

Conditioning Variables: Factors Affecting Adjustment to Residential Relocation

Available evidence suggests that some individuals experience increased levels of social adjustment after residential relocation, others find relocation a stressful life event that involves negative outcomes, and still others are unaffected by a change in residence. These findings indicate the need to identify appropriate conditioning variables—factors that either affect the perception of stress or facilitate or impede adjustment to residential relocation. Although more research is needed to specify the entire range of variables that affect adjustment to residential relocation, available research suggests that there are three classes of conditioning variables: social status variables, personal resources, and situational factors. These variables are discussed in the following paragraphs.

Social Status Variables. Social status variables serve as indicators of position and location in a social structure and, therefore, represent important aspects of life experience. Although there are numerous social status variables that are potentially related to adjustment to residential relocation, previous research has documented the impact of only two such variables. First, Storandt, Wittels, and Botwinick (1975) reported that higher levels of education are conducive to better adjustment to relocation. This pattern holds true for both movers and nonmovers. Second, higher socioeconomic status, which refers primarily to occupational background, has been related to better adjust-

---

ment to residential relocation. Storandt and her associates (1975) maintained that higher socioeconomic status is conducive to better adjustment. Again, this relationship is true of both movers and nonmovers. Moreover, Rosow (1967) found that patterns of adjustment to relocation are influenced by social class. Working-class older persons (individuals who retired from blue-collar jobs) appear to be dependent on the social and physical characteristics of the immediate residential environment, whereas middle-class or white-collar persons are more likely to be oriented to relationships and resources in the broader community.

There is a clear need to examine a greater variety of social status variables as possible factors in the process of adjustment to residential relocation. Age, gender, marital status, and race or ethnic membership are examples of social status variables in need of further study. At this point, we've determined that high levels of education and socioeconomic status generally facilitate social adjustment during later life.

Personal Resources. A social support system that is able to provide both tangible resources and emotional sustenance during times of need is a valuable personal resource—one that facilitates adjustment to many life events, including residential relocation. Available research suggests that warm relationships with relatives and meaningful friendships facilitate adjustment to relocation (Hochschild, 1973; Rosow, 1967; Sherman, 1975a, 1975b; Teaff, Lawton, Nahemow, & Carlson, 1978). It also appears that relationships with one group (family or friends) aren't simply substituted; that is, it doesn't appear that older people who are unable to maintain close relationships with their children turn instead to a peer group for social support. Instead, most older people desire meaningful social bonds with *both* family and friends (Hochschild, 1973). The maintenance of social bonds with both groups is conducive to better social adjustment. Residential relocation can alter interaction with family members and friends, but it's more likely to disrupt friendship patterns. Consequently, in order to adjust to relocation, older individuals need to maintain existing friendship networks or develop peer bonds in their new communities.

Social support is one kind of personal resource that can help to mediate the potentially stressful aspects of residential relocation. Other resources, such as health and financial assets, also influence adjustment to relocation. Thus far, research investigators haven't determined the effects of other personal resources on adjustment to residential relocation. Clearly, there is need for further research in this area.

Situational Factors. Three types of situational factors affect adjustment to residential relocation: the physical characteristics of the new residential environment, the age density of the new residential environment, and the way in which an individual perceives the change in residence (voluntary or involuntary).

It probably isn't surprising that the physical characteristics of the new residential environment influence personal adjustment to residential relocation. Some people are able to move to improved physical surroundings, whereas others must settle for less satisfying residences. Several authors report that issues of space, privacy, and convenience are important to adjustment to residential relocation (Blonsky, 1975; Lawton, Brody, & Turner-Massey, 1978; Lawton, Nahemow, & Teaff, 1975). Many available studies focus on persons entering residences especially designed for older people (retirement villages or federally sponsored housing for the aged, for example). Much of this housing is suited to the physical and social needs of older people and facilitates adjustment to residential relocation. Such physical surroundings can help to offset the potentially stressful aspects of moving to a new home.

The age structure of the new neighborhood also appears to influence adjustment to residential relocation. At one time, researchers predicted that the concentration of older persons in apartment buildings and neighborhoods would hinder personal adjustment. Residential age segregation was expected to generate increased isolation and loneliness for older persons. It was also assumed that older people would resist age segregation and resent the decreased opportunities for developing relationships with younger people.

In fact, available evidence strongly suggests that high proportions of older residents facilitate the development of friendship networks and adjustment to residential relocation (Bultena & Wood, 1969; Hochschild, 1973; Teaff, Lawton, Nahemow & Carlson, 1978). In a now classic study, Rosow (1967) examined the effects of residential age density on friendship networks among 1200 older middle-class and working-class residents of several hundred apartment buildings in Cleveland, Ohio. Residential areas were placed in three categories: (1) normal (1%-15% older population), (2) concentrated (33%-49% older population), and (3) dense (50% or more older population). Although patterns differed according to social class, age, marital status, and gender, the greater the density of older persons in a residential area, the greater the average number of friendships reported by the older residents. The relationship between age density, social class, and number of new friends is shown in Table 7-2. As the table indicates, this relationship was especially strong among working-class respondents. In addition, friendships among the very old, the unmarried, and women were greatly influenced by the age density of the residential area.

Friendships tend to be based on common interests and social homogeneity—similarity in basic social status variables such as age, sex, race, and social class. Consequently, relocation to an environment with a relatively high proportion of age peers facilitates the development of new friendships and is conducive to better personal adjustment to residential relocation. Most housing units that are designed specifically for older people meet the physical needs of older residents. Such housing projects, then, tend to meet both the physical and social needs of older people.

TABLE 7-2. *Number of New Friends in Past Year, by Social Class and Residential Density.*

	Number of New Friends		
	None	1–3	4 or More
Working Class			
Normal	59%	22%	19%
Dense	30	14	56
Middle Class			
Normal	55	19	26
Concentrated	57	17	26
Dense	51	18	31

From *Social Integration of the Aged,* by I. Rosow. Copyright © 1967 by The Free Press, a Division of The Macmillan Company. Reprinted by permission.

The nature of relocation (voluntary or involuntary) has a direct impact on various adaptive outcomes of relocation. (Schulz & Brenner, 1977). As I noted earlier, two studies reported declines in personal well-being as a result of residential relocation (Brand & Smith, 1974; Kasteler, Gray, & Carruth, 1968), whereas other studies reported that personal well-being either improves after relocation or appears to be unaffected by a change in residence. The studies that reported decreases in personal well-being examined older persons who were forced to relocate. Members of the sample studied by Brand and Smith were forced to move as a result of urban renewal. The individuals who participated in the study by Kasteler and his associates were forced to move because of road construction. Similarly, only two studies reported poorer health among those who relocated. The Brand and Smith study, which involved involuntary relocation as a result of urban renewal, was one of these. In the other study (Lawton & Cohen, 1974), it appeared that those who relocated were originally in poorer health than nonmovers and, in fact, sought special housing in which medical services were provided. As Schulz and Brenner (1977) note, the distinction between voluntary and involuntary relocation explains differences in subsequent adjustment: negative outcomes are strongly related to involuntary relocation.

In summary, although only a relatively small number of factors that affect adjustment to residential relocation in later life have been identified thus far, some important factors can be specified. Personal resources, especially social support systems and high levels of education, are conducive to successful adjustment to residential relocation. The physical and social characteristics of the new residential environment also affect personal adjustment. The more pleasant the environment, and the higher the proportion of age peers in the residential area, the more easily adjustment is achieved. Finally, involuntary relocation is a strong predictor of perceptions of stress and adaptive problems.

The Process of Adjustment to Residential Relocation

Most studies of residential relocation in later life compare movers with nonmovers. Few studies monitor levels of adjustment over a period of time. This kind of longitudinal examination is essential to an understanding of the *process* of adjustment to residential relocation. Levels of adjustment should be compared before and after relocation; short-term effects might differ from long-term effects.

Two studies that examined adjustment to residential relocation over a period of time make it possible to assess the process involved. The first study examined older persons who voluntarily moved from independent community residences to a new high-rise apartment building that was specifically designed for older people (Storandt & Wittels, 1975; Storandt, Wittels, & Botwinick, 1975; Wittels & Botwinick, 1974). A comparison group of nonmovers, some of whom were on the waiting list for the new apartment building, was also examined. Four areas of function related to personal adjustment were studied: cognitive and psychomotor performance, health status, levels of activity, and morale and related measures of personal well-being. All participants were eligible for federally sponsored low-income housing and had limited financial assets. They were examined twice—five months prior to moving and again fourteen months later. The results of this study indicated that there were no significant differences in the four areas of functioning between movers and nonmovers over a period of time. The authors concluded that relocation involves no short-term adverse effects.

Carp (1966, 1975a, 1975b, 1977) studied a group of older perons who moved voluntarily to Victoria Plaza, a residential facility designed specifically for older persons. All participants in Carp's study had applied for admission to this new apartment complex. Subsequently, movers (persons admitted to Victoria Plaza) and nonmovers (applicants who weren't admitted) were examined on three test dates: about six months prior to entrance of the movers, twelve months after the movers entered Victoria Plaza, and eight years after the movers entered the residential facility. Carp examined both the short-term and long-term effects of relocation on health, mortality rates, and morale, as well as related measures of personal well-being. Movers fared better than nonmovers on all three adaptive outcomes in both the short-run and the long-run. Carp concluded that residential relocation to Victoria Plaza had a positive impact on movers and that the benefits they derived from the move were still identifiable eight years after their relocation. Carp appropriately noted that, in this study, relocation was voluntary and typically resulted in improved physical surroundings.

Although these longitudinal studies suggest that relocation either improves personal well-being or at least doesn't lead to negative outcomes, caution must be exercised in generalizing from these studies. In both of these studies, relocation was voluntary, resulted in genuine improvements in physical surroundings, and involved residential facilities that are designed for older people. There is a clear need for additional longitudinal studies that trace the process of adjustment to relocation in situations in which individuals move involuntarily or move to unsatisfactory physical surroundings.

Using the Social Stress Model to Understand Adjustment to Relocation

In order to assess the usefulness of the social stress model in understanding adjustment to residential relocation, we need to determine how well the model can accommodate the findings of previous studies. Figure 7-1 presents the social stress model as a model of adjustment to community-based residential relocation. In general, the results of previous studies appear to be quite compatible with a social stress perspective. Residential relocation has been examined from the perspective of several outcomes that are relevant to personal adjustment and well-being. In addition, a number of variables that determine the conditions under which residential relocation is likely to generate a negative outcome have been identified.

Residential relocation in later life usually has a relatively mild impact. In spite of the potentially stressful aspects of residential relocation in terms of disrupted behavior patterns and a sense of loss, most older people who change residences apparently do not suffer appreciable maladjustment. Relocation is usually a low-impact event because most people move voluntarily and obtain housing that they perceive as better than the housing they leave behind. Under certain circumstances, of course (primarily, involuntary relocation to poorer quality housing), residential relocation can have a negative impact on personal well-being.

The social stress model can be used to identify areas that are in need of further inquiry. At this point, nothing is known about the impact of personality factors, anticipatory socialization, and the use of specific, behavioral coping strategies on adjustment to residential relocation. Since these factors affect other life transitions, an examination of their influence on adjustment to residential relocation is certainly needed. In addition, longitudinal studies of the process of adjustment to residential relocation need to be extended to include more diverse samples.

Institutional Relocation

In 1977, approximately 4.6% of the U. S. population age 65 and older were residents of nursing homes, rest homes, and similar institutions (Ingram & Barry, 1977). Although this represents a small proportion of the older population, nearly a million older people reside in institutional settings in the

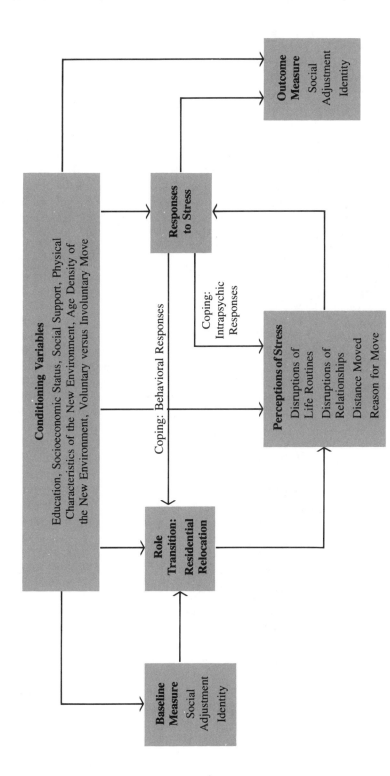

FIGURE 7-1 Adjustments to community-based residential relocation: A social stress model.

U.S. Furthermore, this number doesn't include all of the older individuals who will experience institutionalization. The best available estimates suggest that approximately 25% of all older persons are institutionalized for at least a short period of time (Palmore, 1976) and 20% of all deaths occur in institutional settings (Ingram & Barry, 1977; Kastenbaum & Candy, 1973). Finally, it is clear that the number of older individuals in institutions is increasing steadily. For example, between 1960 and 1970, there was a 58% increase in the number of older individuals residing in institutions. During this same period, the older population increased by only 21% (Pollak, 1976). Such increases in the use of institutions by older persons are expected to continue. Institutionalization has become a relatively common experience of later life.

Institutionalization is not random. The very old (Tobin & Lieberman, 1976), the financially disadvantaged (Barney, 1977; Tobin & Lieberman, 1976), and women (Palmore, 1976) are especially likely to become institutional residents. Older White persons are far more likely to be institutionalized than members of racial or ethnic minorities. In the U.S., for example, only about 6% of all institutionalized older persons are nonwhites (Soldo, 1977).

These demographic correlates of institutionalization might make a great deal of sense if they reflected increased impairment among various subgroups of the population—impairments that require the services and medical care available in institutional settings. To some degree, this may be true. The very old, for example, are likely to be the most impaired segment of the older population. However, several studies suggest that degree of impairment is *not* the best predictor of institutionalization. Rather, the absence of a viable social support system and the corollary condition of living alone are more dependable predictors of institutionalization than degree of impairment (Barney, 1977; Brody, Poulshock, & Masciocchi, 1978; Tobin & Lieberman, 1976). Therefore, the very old, who are more likely to be widowed and whose children might be relatively old, are more likely to be institutionalized: they lack social support systems and suffer increased physical impairment. Racial and ethnic differences in rates of institutionalization appear to reflect subcultural preferences rather than differences in degree of impairment. It appears that older ethnic and Black people are more likely than Whites to remain in the community (cared for by family members and other social support groups), regardless of their level of impairment (Eribes & Bradley-Rawls, 1978).

Perceptions of Stress During Institutionalization

Probably no one welcomes institutionalization. Available evidence uniformly indicates that older people view institutionalization with resignation and dread. Some of the reasons for their general reluctance to enter an institution are obvious. Old-age institutions exist in order to provide a variety of self-care and medical services to people who are unable to care for themselves —at least in the short-run. Consequently, the decision to enter an institution is a public demonstration that one is no longer competent—personally or in terms of mobilizing other resources—to care for oneself. It's difficult for older individuals to acknowledge this degree of dependency. Most of them have been relatively self-sufficient, and they value independence as a cornerstone of personal well-being (Louis Harris & Associates, 1975).

Entering an institution involves a considerable forfeit of personal freedom and privacy. The individual no longer controls his or her immediate surroundings or personal schedule. Many personal possessions must be left behind. Simple decisions such as what to eat and when are no longer a matter of personal choice. Privacy is often severely limited; one must adjust to smaller quarters and a roommate. Although most nursing homes attempt to provide comfortable environments for their residents and serve the personal needs of each individual, older people who enter such institutions are no longer able to routinely make their own decisions. The price they pay for an environment that provides essential services is a considerable loss of autonomy.

In the first section of this chapter, I discussed community-based moves and indicated that such moves are likely to be perceived as at least somewhat stressful due to: (1) disruption of established behavior patterns and routines, (2) disruption of social relationships, and (3) a sense of loss experienced as a result of leaving an emotionally significant physical and social environment. These factors are even more potent during institutionalization; that is, the *degree* of change, disruption, and emotional loss is greater during institutionalization than during a community-based change in residence.

I also noted earlier that involuntary community-based moves are more likely than voluntary moves to be perceived as stressful and to have a negative impact on personal adjustment. The overwhelming majority of institutional moves are involuntary—perceived as moves for which there are no viable alternatives.

In summary, institutional relocation is usually perceived as a stressful life transition for which there is no alternative. It is characterized by loss of independence and freedom and disruption of established behavior patterns and social relationships.

The Impact of Institutional Relocation on Adjustment and Identity

Research has focused on two types of institutional relocation: (1) relocation from the community to an institution, and (2) relocation from one institution to another. Institutionalization—relocation from the community to an institution—usually occurs when an individual can no longer perform self-care tasks or requires medical care and cannot mobilize family members or friends to provide that care. Relocation from one institution to another, which occurs less frequently, can take place for a variety of reasons, the most common of which is the mass transfer of institutional residents to different facilities. In both types of institutional relocation, the older persons involved tend to be a frail and vulnerable group.

Two primary types of research design have been used to examine the impact of institutional relocation. In one common research strategy, movers (persons who either enter an institution or are transferred from one institution to another) are compared with nonmovers (persons who remain in a community or institution). One potential flaw in these studies is that movers and nonmovers might differ in a number of important ways; consequently, differences between the two groups aren't necessarily due to the effects of institutional relocation. A second alternative is a longitudinal study that compares the same individuals before and after relocation. The problem with this design is that the effects of relocation cannot be distinguished from other time-related changes, such as aging and the effects of disease. The best design would combine these strategies and monitor change over time among two groups of older persons.

In the following paragraphs, we will examine available evidence concerning the impact of institutional relocation on adjustment and identity. Unfortunately, very few available studies include both comparisons of movers and nonmovers and longitudinal measurements; consequently, present findings are most appropriately viewed as suggestive rather than conclusive.

Social Adjustment. Health is an important component of social adjustment. Good health facilitates both the successful negotiation of environmental demands and personal perceptions of well-being. Two longitudinal studies provide evidence regarding changes in health subsequent to relocation from the community to an institution. Spasoff and his associates (1978) reported short-term (after one month) improvements in health among nursing-home residents, but their long-term examinations (one year after their subjects entered the institution) revealed significant health deterioration. The authors speculate that the short-term improvements represent immediate gains experienced as a result of increased care, whereas the long-term health deterioration is a result of the inevitable progressions of chronic diseases and the clinical presentation of new chronic conditions. Similarly, Tobin and Lieberman (1976) found that individuals' health remains stable immediately after they enter a nursing home (during the first two months), but it deteriorates after one year. Studies that examine the effects of relocation from one institution to another uniformly report subsequent declines in health (Bourestom & Tars, 1974; Marlowe, 1974; Pino, Rosica, & Carter, 1978). Research findings suggest that institutional relocation—either from the community to an institution or from one institution to another—is typically accompanied by some health deterioration. Because of the rather lengthy time lag between relocation and health deterioration, however, it's impossible to say whether the changes in health are directly or solely attributable to relocation.

Three studies have examined mortality rates among older persons who move into nursing homes or similar institutions. All of these studies conclude that relocation is followed by high mortality rates (Blenkner, 1967; Ferrari, 1963; Tobin & Lieberman, 1976). Before we accept this conclusion as fact, however, we need to examine two issues. First, researchers have identified a number of conditioning variables that help to explain variations in death rates following institutional relocation. Second, the choice of a standard by which to evaluate death rates is problematic. For example, older persons who enter institutions exhibit higher death rates than persons of similar age who remain in the community, and institutional residents are probably more physically impaired than community residents. Therefore, available findings indicate that institutionalization is *related to* a negative outcome, but these findings don't provide definitive evidence that relocation and institutionalization *cause* a negative outcome.

A much larger number of studies have examined mortality rates following relocation from one institution to another. In these studies, an appropriate standard of comparison is usually available. In some cases, movers can be compared with residents who weren't moved; in other cases, death rates after relocation are compared with death rates prior to relocation. The majority of these studies report increased mortality rates following relocation from one institution to another (Aldrich & Mendkoff, 1964; Bourestom & Tars, 1974; Killian, 1970; Marlowe, 1974; Pino, Rosica, & Carter, 1978). In spite of this general pattern, a few studies report no difference in mortality rates between movers and nonmovers or before and after relocation (Gutman & Herbert, 1976; Kowalski, 1978; Markson & Cummings, 1974). One study, in which movers received extensive preparation, reported a slight decrease in death rates after relocation (Zweig & Csank, 1975). Again, we will see later that variations in mortality rates can be explained in part by conditioning variables.

The subjective component of social adjustment is the perception of personal well-being. Although a few authors have examined levels of life satisfaction, morale, and similar social-psychological states related to a sense of well-being among institutionalized older people, current evidence is somewhat ambiguous. Several studies indicate that older persons who reside in institutions report lower levels of life satisfaction and personal well-being than older community residents (Shrut, 1965; Tobin & Lieberman, 1976). However, this pattern could reflect differences in health rather than the effects of institutionalization.

Tobin and Lieberman's longitudinal study (1976) examined one group of persons before and after they entered a nursing home and simultaneously monitored changes among a group of older community residents who did not experience institutionalization. The group of older persons who entered nursing homes consistently exhibited lower levels of life satisfaction both *before and after* institutionalization. Furthermore, life satisfaction did not change significantly after institutionalization; instead, it remained quite stable. Morris (1975), on the other hand, found general increases in life satisfaction among new institutional residents. Therefore, the impact of institutional relocation on perceptions of personal well-being remains a relatively unsettled issue.

Identity. Overall, little attention has been devoted to the impact of institutional relocation on self-concept, self-esteem, and identity. Findings from the single longitudinal study that examined self-esteem over the course of relocation from a community to a nursing home indicate that self-esteem remains relatively stable during this transition. However, relocated persons exhibited lower levels of self-esteem prior to and after institutionalization than persons who remained community residents (Tobin & Lieberman, 1976).

Other available evidence concerning self-concept and self-esteem among institutionalized older persons is not directly linked to the issue of relocation. Wolk and Telleen (1976) compared levels of self-acceptance between residents of a highly structured institution and residents of a less structured institution. They found that self-acceptance was significantly higher among residents of the less structured institution. This finding suggests that dependency and loss of freedom hinder a positive sense of self. Anderson (1967) compared levels of self-esteem between residents of a nursing home and applicants to that nursing home who were awaiting admission. There was no significant difference in self-esteem between those two groups, Gordon and Vinacke (1971) asked nursing-home residents to rate themselves according to effectiveness, independence, and personal acceptability. Subjects in this study used two time referents—the present (institutionalization) and the past (before institutionalization). In all three areas, respondents consistently rated themselves more positively in the past.

Finally, Kaas (1978) reminds us that certain dimensions of identity can change dramatically as a result of institutionalization. Kaas examined attitudes toward sexuality among staff and residents of a nursing home. Although the staff reported high levels of tolerance toward sexual expression by nursing-home residents, the residents themselves indicated that they perceived themselves as sexually unattractive. They weren't interested in sexual activity and expression, and they indicated that sexual identity was no longer important to them. Residents also indicated that lack of privacy stifled any sexual interests they might experience. It appears, then, that sexual identity is altered as a consequence of institutionalization.

Although available evidence is fragmentary, it seems certain that the process of becoming heavily dependent on others for care and medical attention has an impact on self-esteem and identity. It isn't clear, however, whether institutional relocation has a direct impact on identity over and above the impact of loss of independence that is a result of health and self-care deterioration. Clearly, this issue merits further research.

Conditioning Variables: Factors That Affect Adjustment to Institutional Relocation

A variety of factors, or variables, affect adjustment to institutional relocation. These conditioning variables help us to understand the circumstances under which institutional relocation is stressful and why individuals react differently to the same life event. Five classes of variables that affect the impact of institutional relocation have been identified in previous research: social status variables, personal resources, personality factors related to coping, socializing experiences, and situational factors. Each of these classes of conditioning variables will be discussed in the following paragraphs.

Social Status Variables. As I noted earlier, a number of demographic, or social status variables, are correlated with the probability of being institutionalized during later life. In the U.S., the very old, the widowed and unmarried, the financially disadvantaged, women, and Whites are overrepresented in institutions (compared to their numbers in the older population as a whole). Although demographic and social status variables are significant predictors of institutionalization, they do not appear to directly influence adjustment to institutional relocation.

Personal Resources. Two types of personal resources influence adjustment to institutional relocation: physical and cognitive resources and social support systems. Tobin and Lieberman (1976) found that physical health and cognitive abilities can facilitate the transition from community resident to institutional resident. Lieberman (1975) points out that physical and cognitive resources don't *guarantee* successful adjustment: "Inadequate resources predict maladaptation, but adequate resources do not necessarily predict successful adaptation. The resources set the floor on the adaptation process" (p. 154). Relocation from one institution to another usually has a stronger negative impact on persons who suffer from poor health (Pino, Rosica, & Carter, 1978).

The scope and quality of available social support networks also affects adjustment to the transition from community resident to institutional resident. Most nursing-home residents maintain frequent contact with their families and friends (Miller & Beer, 1977), and family visits contribute to adjustment to institutional living arrangements (Noelker & Harel, 1978). Relationships with family members and friends serve as a source of continuity to older persons who experience the pervasive discontinuities that result from institutional relocation. Most nursing-home residents also develop friendships with staff and other residents (Miller & Beer, 1977). These friendships tend to be based on complementary personality characteristics and mutual interests. Although institution-based friendships are usually less intimate than relationships with family members and other friends, pleasant social relationships within institutional environments facilitate adjustment to relocation.

Personality Factors Related to Coping. Tobin and Lieberman (1976) reported that a configuration of personality characteristics, including aggression, hostility, an assertive approach to the environment, and narcissism, is related to long-term survival among nursing-home residents. Although it might seem surprising that such unpleasant personality characteristics are conducive to survival, remember that we are discussing vulnerable older people facing adaptation to environmental change. If this finding can be replicated in a variety of studies, the results will prove significant to mental-health services for the institutionalized aged. As Lieberman (1975) notes, the results of this study imply that conventional perspectives regarding mental health may not apply to institutionalized older persons.

Socializing Experiences. Several studies of relocation of older residents from one institution to another indicate that, when residents are prepared for the move, they are better able to adjust to a new institution. Such preparation has been shown to decrease mortality rates (Jasnau, 1967; Pastalan, 1976; Zweig & Csank, 1975), decrease health deterioration, and increase levels of life satisfaction (Pino, Rosica, & Carter, 1978). In some of these studies, an experimental design was used. Comparisons were made between residents who received preparation for relocation and those who did not. In other studies, patient records were compared before and after relocation. There is a clear need for more research on this topic. We need to develop effective preparation programs. A study by Pastalan (1976) suggests that: (1) individual preparation is more effective than group preparation, and (2) the effectiveness of relocation-preparation programs depends, in part, on the personal characteristics of the individuals who are relocated.

Theoretically, it also should be possible to provide preparation programs for older persons who are moving from a community to an institution. Indeed, many nursing homes encourage prospective residents to visit the institution and become familiar with its policies and services. At this point, however, we have no evidence regarding the effectiveness of such socializing experiences.

Situational Factors. As I noted earlier in this chapter, the distinction between voluntary and involuntary relocation is strongly related to adjustment to community-based relocation: involuntary moves are more likely to be perceived as stressful and to have a negative effect on personal well-being. Since most institutional relocations (either from a community to an institution or from one institution to another) are involuntary, decreased levels of adjustment among institutional residents might reflect, in part, the effects of an unwanted transition. Ferrari (1963) has empirically compared the effects of voluntary and involuntary relocation from a community to an institution. He compared a group of older people who entered an institution voluntarily with a group of older people who were institutionalized involuntarily. Differences in mortality rates during the first ten weeks of residence in the institution were dramatic: 94% of the group who moved involuntarily died during that period, compared to less than 3% of the group who moved voluntarily. Although the results from a single study must be viewed with caution, it appears that, because most institutional relocations are involuntary, older people find it especially difficult to adjust to the changes involved in such relocations.

In summary, although institutional relocation frequently generates significant problems for older individuals, researchers have identified some factors that facilitate adjustment to such relocation. A number of social-status variables are significant correlates of institutionalization, but they don't directly influence the process of adjustment to institutional relocation. Personal resources, including physical health and the social support provided by family members and friends, also facilitate adjustment. Somewhat surprisingly, an aggressive and demanding personality is conducive to survival in long-term-care institutions. There is limited, but pervasive evidence that preparation for relocation can help to offset some of the problems associated with institutional moves. Finally, the fact that most institutional relocations are involuntary, or at least are perceived as such, contributes to perceptions of stress among older individuals and probably hinders their adjustment.

The Process of Adjustment to Institutional Relocation

In order to understand adjustment to institutional relocation clearly we need to compare levels of adjustment before and after relocation and determine whether the short-term effects of relocation differ from the long-term consequences. As I noted earlier, longitudinal studies are the preferred design for examining change over a period of time. Three longitudinal studies have examined the process of adjustment to relocation from a community to an institution. One longitudinal study examined the impact of relocation from one institution to another on personal adjustment.

Relocation from a Community to an Institution.   Morris (1975) examined changes in morale (over a one-year period) among older persons who had been admitted to a nursing home. The results indicated that morale generally increased during the one-year period. Morris also examined the relationship between morale and the appropriateness of the institutional placement (as judged by clinical raters). Those persons who had been placed in an environment that provided appropriate services experienced increases in morale during the one-year period. Increases in morale were not observed among the smaller number of individuals who had been placed in inappropriate institutional settings. This examination of the impact of institutionalization on adjustment is rather limited. We lack information about the participants' levels of adjustment prior to institutionalization, and we can't evaluate the influences of perceptions of stress or conditioning variables. However, this study sensitizes us to the issue of person/environment fit—in this case, the appropriateness of the institution and the services it provides.

Spasoff and his associates (1978) examined adjustment to institutionalization among a group of older Canadians. Components of adjustment included in the study were life satisfaction and health. Data were collected prior to institutionalization and at intervals of one month and one year thereafter. Life satisfaction remained relatively high at all test dates. Health improved one month after relocation but deteriorated noticeably by the end of the year. In addition, 25% of the sample died by the end of the first year. During the one-year period of the study, 15% of the participants were moved to other institutional settings. The results of this study clearly indicate that long-term patterns of adjustment differ from short-term patterns and that some components of adjustment change over a period of time, while others remain stable.

The works of Lieberman and Tobin (Lieberman, 1975; Tobin & Lieberman, 1976) constitute the major available longitudinal examination of the impact of institutionalization on adjustment and identity in later life. In order to isolate the effects of institutionalization itself, three samples were monitored over a period of time: (1) a *relocation sample* that was measured before (while on a waiting list for admission) and after relocation from the community to an institution, (2) an *institutional sample* of persons who had been residents of an institution for one to three years, and (3) a *community sample* of persons who remained in the community during the course of the study. Five components of adjustment and identity—physical health, cognitive functioning, emotional states, affective responsiveness, and self-perception—were measured at three points thought to be critical for the relocation sample: prior to institutionalization, two months after relocation, and one year after relocation. The institution and community samples were measured at comparable intervals.

Perhaps the most important finding of Tobin and Lieberman's study is that *prior to institutionalization,* the relocation sample resembled the institutional sample more than the community sample. Table 7-3 shows the mean values for the three samples on a variety of measures related to adjustment and identity. (These measures were taken before the relocation sample was institutionalized.) A comparison of the means across the three samples reveals the similarities between the relocation sample and the institutional sample. These findings indicate that, among individuals in the relocation sample, levels of adjustment and identity were relatively low prior to institutionalization. Tobin and Lieberman suggest that these low levels of adjustment and identity among older persons awaiting admission to institutions reflect the precipitating events that lead to institutionalization (health deterioration or loss of social support,

TABLE 7-3. *Means on Measures of Social Psychological Functioning for Community, Relocation, and Institutional Samples.*

Area of Functioning	Community Sample	Relocation Sample	Institutional Sample
Cognitive functioning			
Orientation	.7%	1.3%	1.7%
Time estimate	23.2	21.8	26.4
Retention	7.6	12.6	16.2
Organization	27.3	34.5	35.2
Perceptual accuracy	27.9	21.8	22.1
Originality	10.2	9.4	9.9
Signs of cognitive			
inadequacy	.5	1.4	1.0
Affective responsiveness			
Range of affects	5.8	4.3	5.2
Willingness to			
introspect	3.4	2.1	1.8
Emotional states			
Well-being	19.2	15.8	16.8
Hope	.7	− .9	− .4
Anxiety	15.3	19.8	16.2
Depression	7.6	13.9	12.3
Self-perception			
Perception—self-care			
inadequacy	.8	2.3	2.7
Self-esteem	23.2	19.2	18.3
Adequacy	3.9	− .83	1.8
Dominance	.34	− .21	.31
Affiliation	.08	.16	.09

From *Last Home for the Aged,* by S. S. Tobin and M. A. Lieberman. Copyright 1976 by Jossey-Bass, Inc., Publishers. Reprinted by permission.

for example) and the perceptions of stress that accompany the decision to enter an institution. At any rate, these findings suggest that the differences between older community residents and older institutional residents aren't due solely to the influence of institutionalization.

Tobin and Lieberman found that the effects of relocation from a community to an institution are most acute during the initial stages of institutionalization. Although levels of adjustment and identity remain relatively stable for two months, some perceptions of stress were reported by the relocation sample. Interviews with participants indicated increased preoccupation with feelings of loss, and relocation-related problems were frequently mentioned —problems such as lack of privacy and conflicts with roommates.

The follow-up study, which was conducted one year after relocation, indicated considerable deterioration among both the relocation and institutional samples. In the relocation sample, 33% of the individuals suffered marked deterioration in functioning, and 15% of them had died. One-half of the institutional sample had either deteriorated or died. In contrast, only 20% of the community sample experienced severe deterioration or death.

Tobin and Lieberman's work is an invaluable contribution to our understanding of the impact of institutionalization on adjustment and identity. Their data strongly suggest that the primary influences on adjustment and identity are factors that *precipitate* institutionalization. In addition, they demonstrate that most older persons who experience institutionalization lack the personal resources that most of us use to offset the stressful aspects of life transitions. In other words, institutionalization is a major disruption that is experienced by those older persons who are least likely to be able to cope with relocation.

Relocation from One Institution to Another. Bourestom and Tars (1974) examined the effects of relocation from one nursing home to another on mortality rates and health. Their study included three samples: (1) a *radical-change sample* of individuals who were moved to a larger facility in another community, (2) a *moderate-change sample* of individuals who were moved to a new building in the same facility, and (3) a *control sample* of individuals who weren't relocated. (The radical-change and moderate-change samples were relocated involuntarily.) Data were collected one month prior to relocation and at intervals of 1, 4, 8, and 12 months after relocation. At 6 months, differences in mortality rates were dramatic: 26% of the control group had died, 37% of the moderate-change group had died, and 43% of the radical-change group had died. Higher death rates were observed among members of the radical-change group prior to relocation, suggesting anticipatory stress. Moreover, their self-perceptions of health decreased after relocation. This study makes a unique contribution in that the effects of environmental change are examined, while the involuntary nature of those changes remains constant. Bourestom and Tars suggest that the degree of environmental change resulting from relocation is directly related to the probability of negative outcomes.

Using the Social Stress Model to Understand Adjustment to Institutional Relocation

As Figure 7-2 indicates, the social stress model provides a useful framework for understanding the process of adjustment to institutional relocation. The findings of previous studies are compatible with the concepts of the social stress perspective and the process it implies. The variety of conditioning variables identified in previous studies is particularly noteworthy, since these variables help us to understand the conditions under which institutional relocation is likely to have a negative impact on personal adjustment and identity.

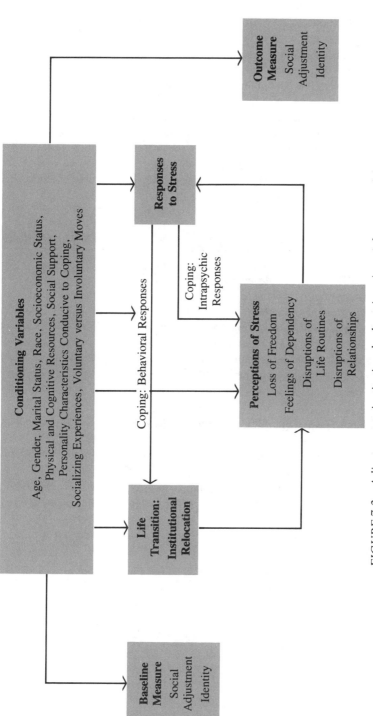

FIGURE 7-2 *Adjustment to institutional relocation: A social stress model.*

The importance of examining life transitions as *processes* is illustrated by the examination of institutional relocation. Although longitudinal data concerning this topic remain relatively rare, several studies, especially those of Lieberman and Tobin, suggest that the negative effects of institutional environments are less severe than had previously been assumed. Much of the deterioration in health, and many of the general adaptive problems characteristic of institutionalized older persons, apparently exist prior to institutionalization and operate as a major determinant of institutionalization. These studies don't discount the very real stresses that accompany institutionalization. Indeed, institutionalization, along with widowhood, appears to be one of the most dreaded transitions of later life. However, the point is that institutionalization is a *consequence* of adaptive problems as well as a *cause* of them.

Review Questions

1. *According to available evidence, what are the primary differences between relocation from a community to an institution and relocation from one institution to another?*
2. *What mechanisms and procedures might be used to more effectively socialize older people to institutional relocation?*
3. *Although retirement communities receive considerable publicity, they serve a very small proportion of the older population. In what ways are residents of such communities likely to be unrepresentative of the older population?*
4. *Tobin and Lieberman's study dramatically highlights the importance of examining older persons both before and after relocation. In what ways does this kind of longitudinal study increase our knowledge of the effects of institutionalization on adjustment and identity?*
5. *The federal government invests funds in housing projects for the elderly. In some cases, such housing projects are available to eligible persons of all ages; in other cases, residence is restricted to older persons. Which of these two arrangements is likely to facilitate adjustment among older residents? Why?*

8

Conclusions
and
Implications

We began our investigation of later life with a series of interrelated goals. First, we wanted to understand the nature of role transitions commonly experienced during the second half of adulthood and their effects on personal well-being. Second, we intended to develop a model, or theoretical perspective, that could be used in examining the wide range of role transitions and role changes common during later life. At the same time, we required a model that could incorporate the complexities of adjustment and take into account the fact that role transitions are experienced differently by persons of varying backgrounds and personal and social characteristics. Third, we wanted to assess the usefulness of the social stress model. We chose to do so by examining the model's ability to integrate and clarify existing research findings regarding a number of major role transitions and life events common in late adulthood.

The previous chapters were devoted to the achievement of those goals. The first three chapters identified the elements necessary for an understanding of adjustment to role transitions and life events during late adulthood. We can understand the major adaptive challenges of later life by using the concepts of role transitions and life events, and we can identify the consequences of social stress by examining two components of personal well-being: adjustment and identity. Finally, it was suggested that the complexities of individual responses to stressful situations can be better understood by taking social status factors, personal resources, and coping skills into account. Chapter 4 was devoted to an examination of various models of adjustment to social stress and a presentation of an integrated model. In Chapters 5, 6, and 7, the social stress model was used, in conjunction with available research findings, to examine the major role transitions and role changes in three significant areas of later life: the world of work, the world of the family, and the residential environment.

Our final task is to assess how well we have met our initial objectives. In this chapter, the implications of our examination of social adjustment during later life will be discussed in three contexts. First, the general contributions of the social stress model to our understanding of the consequences of role transitions and life events will be reviewed. Second, we will review the ways in which our application of the social stress model has increased our understanding of adjustment to the major transitions of later life. Finally, the implications of our investigation for policy and practice will be discussed.

Contributions of the Social Stress Model

Overall, the social stress model has provided a useful framework for integrating and clarifying available research findings that focus on adjustments to role transitions common in later life. The model incorporates research findings regarding a number of role transitions, ranging from the relatively low-impact empty-nest transition to the major disruptions of widowhood and institutionalization. The social stress model also was able to take into account the complex range of factors that influence the process of adjustment. Some of the key features of the social stress model are reviewed in the following paragraphs.

The Perception of Stress: Stress is in the Eye of the Beholder

The social stress model, which guided our investigation, emphasizes the perception of stress. The distinction between role transitions or presumed stressors and individuals' perceptions of stress is important for several reasons.

First, from a conceptual viewpoint, the attention to perceptions of stress prevents us from using the concept of stress in a tautological manner. In many previous studies, the impact of role transitions and other life events was related to an outcome without an assessment of the perceptions of stress. Such designs are inherently circular: when negative outcomes were observed, investigators concluded that an event was stressful; when positive outcomes were observed, they concluded that an event wasn't stressful. In such cases, the measure of stress is inherently confounded with that of the outcome. The assessment of perceptions of stress frees us from this circularity by ensuring that stress is measured independently of its consequences.

Second, the incorporation of perceptions of stress into our model permits us to identify those cases in which an event is perceived as stressful but does *not* lead to a negative outcome. Several of the major role transitions of later life are perceived as stressful (individuals experience a sense of loss or disruptions of customary behavior patterns) but do not necessarily lead to major threats to identify or declines in adjustment. Individuals who have adequate resources and coping skills, for example, might perceive a transition as stressful but intervene effectively and avoid a negative outcome. When perceptions of stress aren't taken into account, effective coping strategies are ignored. Since we want to understand adaptive success as well as adaptive failure, examination of perceptions of stress is crucial.

Third, the inclusion of perceptions of stress in our model focuses our attention on the subjective meanings of role transitions and reminds us that different individuals perceive the same role transition or life event in very different ways. The assumption that a given role transition—retirement, for example—has only one meaning is overly simplistic. For some individuals, retirement signals the end of a long-term identity investment; for others, it is a relief. Some transitions—widowhood and institutionalization, for example —appear to be viewed as stressful by virtually everyone; however, there is usually variation in the personal meanings of various transitions. In order to distinguish transitions that are uniformly perceived as stressful from those that vary in meaning from one individual to another, investigators need to examine individuals' perceptions of stress.

When a presumably stressful event is not perceived as stressful, two possible explanations are generally offered. The obvious possibility is that the individual simply doesn't experience stress. The second possibility is that a psychological process of denial occurs. Since individuals are unaware of denial, there is no easy way to determine when it takes place. The most frequently used method is to demonstrate that a life event is related to a negative outcome, even in the absence of perceptions of stress. Unfortunately, this approach identifies only those cases in which denial is an *ineffective* coping strategy.

The influence of cognitive strategies on perceptions of stress has received little attention. The entire topic of how expectations, aspirations, and motivation are related to perceptions of stress merits further attention. Our research review provided several indications that this would be a fruitful area for further inquiry. For example, both marital satisfaction and general life satisfaction of parents are lower while their children are adolescents and are preparing to leave the parental home (see Chapter 6). In spite of this, most middle-aged parents don't attribute their lower levels of satisfaction to the parental role, and they report that they don't regret the child-rearing decision. One possible explanation for this discrepancy is that something other than their relationships with their children leads to lower levels of satisfaction among middle-aged parents. Another possible explanation is that people use a variety of cognitive strategies to deal with perceptions of stress. In other words, parents might view increased conflict with adolescent children as an inherent part of raising children—a problem they are willing to deal with in order to experience the counterbalancing joys of parenthood. Consequently, problems with adolescent children could be viewed as a normal and expected (albeit less rewarding) aspect of parenthood rather than an unexpected stressful life event. Although this example serves as an illustration and a context for speculation, it calls attention to the broader issue of cognitive appraisal. Perhaps some individuals deal effectively with the major transitions common in later life by changing their aspirations and motivations. We need to remember that a discrepancy between the ideal and the real might be more easily resolved by changing our definition of what is ideal than by attempting to change reality.

We also need to remember that people often have apparently contradictory attitudes; this might alter perceptions of stress. For example, many older persons report positive attitudes toward both work and retirement (see Chapter 5). This runs counter to the common notion that commitment to work leads to a negative orientation toward retirement. When work and retirement are perceived as rewarding, the latter may be perceived as nonstressful even by a person who enjoys work. The same sort of process might operate when people who experience residential relocation express regret as well as anticipation. We need to devote more attention to the range of attitudes and cognitions that influence perceptions of stress.

Conditioning Variables: Determining When Stress Does and Does Not Lead to Negative Outcomes

One of the primary lessons we learned during our trek through the major transitions of later life is that an assessment of relevant mediating or conditioning variables is crucial to an understanding of adjustment to role transitions. In order to understand an individual's adjustment to a transition, we need to know the nature of the transition, the meaning of the transition to the individual, the personal resources and coping skills that can be mobilized, the extent to which relevant socialization experiences have taken place, and the temporal aspects of the transition. Role transitions are important life experiences; their effects are heavily dependent on the personal and social qualities of the individual and the context in which the transition occurs.

Our review of adjustment to role transitions in later life suggests that several conditioning variables merit further empirical attention. Specific behavioral coping strategies and socializing experiences in particular have received only limited examination thus far. Since we repeatedly found that whether transitions lead to positive or negative outcomes is largely dependent on the influence of conditioning variables, further empirical inquiry in this area is clearly warranted.

Although a wide variety of specific conditioning variables influence the transitions common in later life, from a conceptual perspective this variety can be subsumed under a limited number of key classes of variables. Personal resources, coping skills, socialization experiences, and social status factors influence adjustment to a broad range of transitions. One of the advantages of the social stress model is that it permits us to observe the complexities of adjustment to transitions, while it keeps the scope of our examination within manageable conceptual limits. In this sense, the social stress model allows us to see the forest as well as the trees.

By examining conditioning variables, we are able to observe the importance of the individual in acting on the environment and shaping his or her life course. Individuals develop resources and mobilize them in times of need, develop and exercise their coping skills, and take advantage of socializing experiences. By examining the impact of these individual responses, the social stress model avoids the implication that the effects of a transition are solely determined by factors external to the person. We live in a capricious environment, but it is an environment on which we can exert some influence.

Adjustment As a Process

The social stress model emphasizes the importance of viewing adjustment to role transitions as a process. As the model clearly indicated, responses to stressful transitions are distinct from the outcomes of those events. In addition, the short-term consequences of a transition sometimes differ from the long-term consequences. For example, the short-term consequences of the death of a spouse differ from the long-term consequences of widowhood (see Chapter 6).

The effects of conditioning variables depend, in part, on the stage of the adjustment process. Therefore the distinction noted in Chapter 3 between anticipatory coping and coping responses refers to the stage of the adjustment process at which coping occurs. Anticipatory coping occurs prior to a transition and is oriented toward alleviating the impact of the transition or perhaps preventing its occurrence. In contrast, coping responses occur after a transition has taken place.

In our review of the major role transitions that are common in later life, we found that the social stress model is best suited to an examination of bounded events or transitions in which one can specify both the occurrence of the transition and an appropriate time at which to assess its impact. For example, the model was not suited to an examination of grandparenthood. Although it's possible to identify the occurrence of this role transition, grandparenthood is the beginning of a long-term, ongoing, and evolving relationship between grandparent and grandchild. In order to keep the study of the process of adjustment within manageable limits, it's important to examine bounded role transitions.

In summary, the social stress model is a valuable tool that can be used to examine adjustment to role transitions and other life events. The model helps us to distinguish between the experience of stress and the consequences of stress, to observe adaptive success as well as adaptive failure, and to undertand the conditions under which a role transition leads to a negative outcome. In addition, the model incorporates elements that permit us to observe the ways in which individuals can actively respond to and alter the impact of transitions. Finally, the social stress model recognizes adjustment to role transitions as a process. We turn now to a discussion of the ways in which our application of the social stress model has increased our understanding of adjustment to the major transitions of later life.

Role Transitions in Later Life: Crisis, Challenge, or Contentment?

In *Why Survive? Being Old in America,* Butler (1975) provides a sensitive and informed discussion of the quality of later life in the U. S. The mere fact that he posed such a question in the title of his book, however, illustrates the crisis orientation that has pervaded social science theory and research concerning later life. From a crisis perspective, old age is viewed as a period of decline and disappointment—a period in which individuals are at the mercy of an environment that is either indifferent or hostile. In addition to this external burden, capacities and energies begin to wane. Role transitions threaten personal well-being, generate a sense of loss, disrupt customary behavior patterns, and sever all ties to social structures.

In contrast to this gloomy perspective, evidence suggests that most older people exhibit adequate levels of adjustment. They successfully negotiate environmental demands, report relatively high levels of life satisfaction, and maintain viable personal identities. In addition, most of the major role transitions that are characteristic of later life do not appear to lead to negative outcomes.

This is not to imply that aging doesn't involve some observable developmental declines or that social structures don't generate problems for older people. Nor is it accurate to conclude that all older persons cope with the stresses of role transitions. Indeed, a portrayal of old age as a time during which one simply reaps the well-deserved rewards of a long life is as overly simplistic as the view of later life as a period characterized by adaptive failure and a decline in personal well-being. The social stress model discourages such "feast or famine" views and focuses on the conditions that determine whether or not role transitions pose major problems for older people.

The role transitions reviewed in this book vary widely in the degree to which they are generally perceived as stressful. Some transitions, such as the empty nest and residential relocation, usually aren't perceived as stressful. Others, such as retirement, appear to generate some degree of stress but generally aren't viewed as traumatic. Still other transitions, such as widowhood and institutionalization, generate a great deal of stress. These patterns describe general reactions to various role transitions in later life. It's important to remember that the meaning of various role transitions varies widely from one individual to another. Some middle-aged persons find the departure of the last child from the parental home a traumatic transition. Similarly, some persons experience much more stress than others as the result of the death of a spouse.

The impact of various conditioning variables greatly influences the process of adjustment to role transitions and life events during later life. In some cases, coping skills, personal resources, and other conditioning variables preclude stress. In cases in which stress is experienced, effective coping and adequate resources either prevent negative outcomes or facilitate recovery from the negative impact of a stressful transition. Adaptive failure occurs when a stressful transition is experienced and resources and coping skills cannot meet the demands of the situation.

Since many older people don't experience negative outcomes as a result of role transitions, it appears that personal resources, coping skills, and socialization experiences often counterbalance the impact of stressful role transitions. In spite of this, older persons tend to have lower levels of resources than younger adults. Some of these relative deprivations, such as declines in health, are inherent to the aging process. Others, such as income reductions that are associated with retirement, reflect common social practices. Still others, such as differences in levels of education, reflect differences among cohorts. The very old are especially likely to suffer multiple resource losses. Rates of adaptive failure subsequent to role transitions can be expected to increase to the degree to which the older population experiences loss of resources, impediments to effective coping, and denial of appropriate socialization experiences. This suggests that the greatest asset in later life is the ability to effectively respond to demands and challenges. It's understandable, then, that the same transition has varying impacts on different individuals: people who lack resources experience adaptive problems regardless of the transition they undergo.

The title of this section posed a question: "Role transitions in later life: crisis, challenge, or contentment?" For the older population as a whole, it appears that role transitions do *not* usually generate crises (negative outcomes), although rates of adaptive failure vary widely, depending on the specific role transition. (Institutionalization, for example, is associated with high rates of maladjustment.) At the individual level, adjustment is related to: (1) the nature of the transition, (2) the resources, coping skills, socialization experiences, and personal characteristics of the individual, and (3) the context in which the transition occurs.

Implications for Policy and Practice

Commitment to public intervention in support of older persons is characteristic of industrialized societies (Binstock & Levin, 1976; Lakoff, 1976). Such commitment is evidenced by both substantial fiscal expenditures on services for the elderly and public support of public intervention for older persons. For example, in the United States, public expenditures in support of older persons are escalating dramatically, leading one observer to describe the patterns of public investment as "the graying of the federal budget" (Hudson, 1978). Although many of us might describe current expenditures as too small, or too piecemeal, there is no doubt that the current level of public investment in services for older persons represents a considerable sum of money. In addition, most adults in the U. S., regardless of age, feel that public programs that ensure quality of life for older persons are both appropriate and desirable (Louis Harris & Associates, 1975). Although the personal sacrifices required to support programs for older persons often generate negative reactions, public endorsement of programs and services for the elderly is strong in industrialized societies.

The process by which public services for the older population are authorized, designed, and implemented is complex. (The description of this process presented here is simplified for purposes of brevity.) At the most basic level, publicly supported services are political phenomena. They are influenced by government officials, bureaucratic administrators, and lobbyists and special-interest groups. Established social-service (or social-intervention) programs typically reflect the political compromises required to assemble sufficient support for policy adoption, regardless of whether the compromises contribute to or detract from the effectiveness, efficiency, and rationality of those programs (Binstock & Levin, 1976; Lakoff, 1976).

Once services have been authorized by government officials, a different set of persons is responsible for designing and implementing the service programs. Program planners design the specific content and methods of service delivery. Practitioners of various kinds are responsible for the delivery of services to older persons. Finally, a third set of professionals evaluate the impact and effectiveness of programs. Although all three groups—planners, practitioners, and evaluators—are bound to and guided by legislated policy, they are concerned with the efficiency, effectiveness, and rationality of service programs.

Where, in this complex process, is the role or potential contribution of social science? Under ideal circumstances, social science theory and research contributes to the process of social intervention in a number of ways. First, all social intervention rests on a conceptualization of what the world is like and what can be done to alter its less desirable qualities (Estes & Freeman, 1976). Consequently, since social scientists systematically observe and study the social world, the information they gather is potentially useful to those groups who authorize and design service programs. Indeed, social science data represent one of the many sources of information used in the political process of policy adoption and authorization. Social scientists testify before congressional hearings, consult with program planners, and provide input for the process of policy development. (It should be noted, however, that social scientists are one of many groups that participate in the political process of policy adoption.) Also, social scientists often help to evaluate the impact of social intervention by applying their theories and measurement skills to the task of determining whether programs have accomplished their stated goals.

A social science research perspective has guided this examination of adjustment to role transitions in later life. My efforts have been devoted to an integration of research findings and the use of social science theory to better understand the major discontinuities and disruptions of later life. Although the emphasis in this book has been placed on integration and synthesis, we should consider the potential implications of these findings with regard to the policy and practice of assisting older people. The patterns discerned here have three primary implications concerning such policy and practice.

First, the social stress model's emphasis on understanding the conditions under which role transitions lead to positive or negative outcomes has relevance for policy planners and practitioners. Since we can identify those older individuals who are most likely to suffer declines in personal well-being or functional capacity as a result of role transitions, we can identify *target groups* that are especially likely to profit from appropriate service intervention. Programs need not be designed for or offered to the entire older population, most of whom do not require services.

As Binstock and Levin (1976) note, the notion of target groups has both advantages and disadvantages. On the positive side, by linking services to appropriate target groups, we can ensure that intervention is: (1) specific to identified service needs, and (2) directed to those persons most in need of services. On the negative side, when target groups are too narrow, it becomes difficult to generate the broad-based political support that is required for policy adoption. Furthermore, the use of target groups can lead to expensive and complex bureaucratic regulations, such as complex eligibility requirements. Therefore, although our research review suggests that we are able to identify those older persons most likely to experience maladaptation as a result of role transitions, the pragmatic use of this ability in policy adoption and implementation is ambiguous.

Second, in order to be useful to policy planners and practitioners, research must address variables that are potentially manipulable in service terms —a requirement that doesn't apply to basic, knowledge-oriented research (Estes & Freeman, 1976). For example, although it might be important to know that smoking during early and middle adulthood is significantly related to respiratory illness in later life, this knowledge contributes little to our ability to design appropriate service interventions for the treatment and management of respiratory illnesses among the older population. The social stress perspective, along with the research review of adjustment to role transitions presented in this book, suggests that, although it might not be realistic to expect to prevent social stress by intervention, it *is* possible to provide services that facilitate adjustment and successful negotiation of stressful role transitions. Many of the role transitions common in later life cannot be prevented. Even the most effective service program cannot ensure freedom from widowhood. Therefore, if our only available information suggested that widowhood generates adaptive problems, we would have little on which to base the design and implementation of effective programs to help people deal with widowhood. However, since we have knowledge of the factors that influence adjustment to role transitions, we can develop effective intervention programs to help individuals adjust to these transitions. Personal resources, coping skills, and socialization experiences all facilitate adjustment to stressful role transitions. Furthermore, in contrast to role transitions, these factors can be manipulated to some degree. Service programs can be (and often are) oriented toward increasing older individual's resources, developing their coping skills, and providing relevant socialization experiences. The social stress model can be used to identify the particular types of services that facilitate adjustment to stressful role transitions in later life.

Finally, policy planners and practitioners can gain valuable information by examining the conditions under which older people effectively negotiate stressful role transitions without intervention. Policy planners and service providers often take an advocacy stance toward their clients and publicize the need for services among particular subgroups of the population. They take such a stance in order to develop public support and assemble the resources they need to plan and implement service programs. In addition, because their efforts are directed toward the neediest older people, planners and practitioners are likely to deal with an unrepresentative segment of the older population. Together, these factors tend to lead to a "social-problem" orientation toward older people—an image of older people as needy or ineffective. As Lakoff

(1976) notes, social policy for the older population is likely to rest on "an exaggerated conception of the incapacities of the elderly" (p. 643). This social-problem orientation is analogous to the crisis orientation of much of the social science literature that focuses on later life. Although such a perspective sensitizes us to the problems of later life, it increases the possibility that the older population will be mistakenly stereotyped as incompetent or overwhelmed by adaptive problems.

We need to provide the benefits of effective service programs to individuals who experience adaptive problems in later life. At the same time, we need to acknowledge the resilience and capabilities of the majority of older persons, who successfully negotiate the transitions of later life and maintain high levels of personal well-being. We need to acknowledge and learn from the strengths and capabilities of our older population and provide help for those older persons who are in need of services—this is a major challenge for all of us.

Review Questions

1. *When we discuss the well-being and adjustment of older people, it is crucial to distinguish between patterns that apply to the older population and those that apply to individuals. Why? What difference does this distinction make?*

2. *A sociologist examines the relationship between retirement and adjustment and reports that retirement is not associated with decreased well-being. He or she concludes that retirement is not a stressful role transition. What is the essential flaw in this design? How could it be corrected?*

3. *If you were asked to recommend intervention policies to facilitate adjustment to widowhood among older people, what kinds of things would you suggest?*

4. *In what ways can older people be viewed as a resource?*

Glossary

---

achieved status: Social positions that individuals occupy as a result of their own efforts, motivations, and competence (such as occupations).

adjustment: A compatible fit between the person and the environment. Successful adaptation is characterized by two conditions: the individual meets the demands of the environment and experiences a sense of general well-being in relation to the environment.

anticipatory socialization: Socialization that occurs in a gradual way, when individuals know that they will (or might) someday occupy a particular position. "Mental rehearsals" can help individuals to prepare for future status occupancy.

ascribed status: Social positions that are socially assigned on the basis of individual or social characteristics, regardless of the efforts or desires of the individual. (Examples include gender and age.)

community-based moves: Residential relocations that take place within the community (as opposed to institutional living quarters). Community-based moves range from moves from one dwelling unit to another to migration to different communities or geographical regions.

coping: The covert and overt behaviors individuals use to prevent, alleviate, or respond to stressful situations. Coping encompasses behaviors that are directed toward altering the perception of stress and emotional distress, as well as efforts to alleviate stressful situations.

empty nest: Departure of the last child from the parental home.

extended family: Family structure in which multiple generations of a family share a single household.

identity: The configuration of self-perceptions and self-evaluations that are subjectively significant to the individual.

institutional relocation: Residential relocations in which individuals move from the community to an institution or from one institution to another. The common element in institutional relocations is that individuals relinquish freedom and autonomy in order to receive the services offered by the institution.

interactionist perspective: A sociological approach that explains social attitudes and behaviors and social structure in terms of subjective perceptions and interpretations. According to this perspective, although social structure provides the context for behavior, individuals behave in accordance with their interpretations and, through their behavior, help to mold and modify social structure.

norms: Norms are socially defined rules or standards of behavior. Norms provide guidelines to the range of attitudes and behaviors appropriate to roles and social situations.

nuclear family: Family structure in which the marital couple and their minor children make up the household composition.

primary socialization: Intense period of socialization experienced in early childhood, during which individuals learn the basic skills, attitudes, and behaviors they need to become members of society.

role: Behavior patterns and expectations associated with a particular status. These behavioral expectations and behaviors include both the rights and responsibilities associated with status occupancy.

role change: Situations in which a status is retained, while role expectations and behaviors change over time or with age.

role-making: The process by which individuals create their own roles. In role-making situations, socialization is the negotiation process by which role behavior patterns are developed.

role shifts: Role shifts are changes in the behavioral expectations related to status occupancy. There are two major types of role shifts: (1) role transitions, in which both a status and its accompanying role are changed, and (2) role changes, in which a status is retained, while role expectations change over time or with age.

role-taking: The process by which individuals acquire predefined roles and are socialized to perform those roles in a conforming manner.

role transitions: Situations in which both the status and its accompanying role are changed (for example, the transition from single person to spouse) or lost (for example, retirement, which represents loss of the work status and role).

secondary socialization: Socialization for specific statuses and roles acquired after primary socialization (for example, the acquisition of occupational skills). In contrast to primary socialization, secondary socialization involves a narrow scope of an individual's skills and attitudes, it takes place in unemotional situations, and it is likely to be voluntary.

self-concept: The cognitive aspects of self-perception—individuals' descriptive perceptions of themselves as objects.

self-esteem: The affective and evaluative aspects of self-perception—judgments made about the self as an object.

significant others: Persons who have the greatest influence on an individual in terms of self-evaluation and conformity to social norms.

social networks: Patterns of social involvement. The configuration of people with whom an individual maintains regular contact and interaction.

social stress: Social stress is a social situation that poses an adaptive challenge or problem to an individual. Social stress does not necessarily lead to a negative outcome, but it requires negotiation by the individual.

social support systems: The members of one's social support networks who can be called upon or mobilized on one's behalf during times of stress or need.

socialization: From the structural perspective, socialization is the process of learning the skills and motivations needed to perform a role. From interactionist perspectives, socialization is viewed as an interactive process of negotiation between socializers and socializees that culminates when both parties develop the attitudes, skills, and personal styles that will be used in enacting roles.

status: A socially defined position in the social structure. A status is the structural counterpart of a social role.

structural perspective: A sociological approach that explains individual and group behavior in terms of objective social structure—that is, by the pattern of relatively stable statuses and roles found in society.

values: Values are abstract, general principles to which members of a group or society feel a strong, emotional commitment. Values are the general standards of behavior on which more specific norms are based.

References

Adams, B. N. The middle-class adult and his widowed or still-married mother. *Social Problems*. 1968a, *16*, 50–59.

Adams, B. N. *Kinship in an urban setting*. Chicago: Markham Publishing Co., 1968b.

Aldous, J. Intergenerational visiting patterns: Variation in boundary maintenance as an explanation. *Family Process*, 1967, 235–251.

Aldrich, C., & Medkoff, E. Relocation of the aged and disabled: A mortality study. *Journal of American Geriatrics Society*, 1963, *11*, 185–194.

Anderson, N. N. Effects of institutionalization on self-esteem. *Journal of Gerontology*, 1967, *22*, 313–317.

Andrews, F. M. & Withey, S. B. *Social indicators of well-being*. New York: Plenum Press, 1976.

Atchley, R. C. Retirement and work orientation. *Gerontologist*, 1971, *11*, 29–32.

Atchley, R. C. Dimensions of widowhood in later life. *Gerontologist*, 1975, *15*, 175–178.

Atchley, R. C. *The sociology of retirement*. Cambridge, Mass.: Schenkman, 1976.

Back, K. W., & Guptill, C. S. Retirement and self-ratings. In I. H. Simpson & J. C. McKinney (Eds.), *Social aspects of aging*. Durham, N. C.: Duke University Press, 1966.

Barfield, R. E., & Morgan, J. *Early retirement: The decision and the experience*. Ann Arbor: Institute for Social Research, 1969.

Barney, J. L. The prerogative of choice in long-term care. *Gerontologist*, 1977, *17*, 309–314.

Berardo, F. Kinship interaction and communications among space-age migrants. *Journal of Marriage and the Family*, 1967, *29*, 541–554.

Berardo, F. M. Survivorship and social isolation: The case of the aged widower. *Family Coordinator*, 1970, *19*, 11–25.

Binstock, R. H., & Levin, M. A. The political dilemmas of intervention policies. In R. H. Binstock & E. Shanas (Eds.), *Handbook of aging and the social sciences*. New York: Van Nostrand Reinhold, 1976.

Binstock, R. H., & Shanas, E. (Eds.). *Handbook of aging and the social sciences*. New York: Van Nostrand Reinhold, 1976.

Blau, Z. S. Structural constraints on friendships in old age. *American Sociological Review*, 1961, *26*, 429–439.

Blenkner, M. Environmental change and the aging individual. *Gerontologist*, 1967, *7*, 101–105.

Blonsky, L. E. The desire of elderly nonresidents to live in a senior citizen apartment building. *Gerontologist*, 1975, *17*, 88–91.

Bornstein, P. E., Clayton, P. J., Halikas, J. A., Maurice, W. L., & Robins, E. The depression of widowhood after thirteen months. *British Journal of Psychiatry*, 1973, *122*, 561–566.

Botwinick, J. *Aging and behavior: A comprehensive integration of research findings*. New York: Springer, 1973.

Bourestom, N., & Tars, S. Alterations in life patterns following nursing home relocation. *Gerontologist*, 1974, *14*, 506–509.

Bourque, L. B., & Back, K. W. Life graphs and life events. *Journal of Gerontology*, 1977, *32*, 669–674.

Bradburn, N. M. The structure of psychological well-being. Chicago: Aldine, 1969.

Brand, F., & Smith, R. Life adjustment and relocation of the elderly. *Journal of Gerontology*, 1974, *29*, 336–340.

Bratthall, K. Flexible retirement and the new Swedish partial-pension scheme. *Industrial Gerontology*, 1976, *2*, 157–166.

Brim, O. G., Jr. Theories of the male mid-life crisis. *The Counseling Psychologist*, 1976, *6*, 2–9.

Brody, E. M., Kleban, M. H., & Liebowitz, B. Intermediate housing for the elderly: Satisfaction of those who moved in and those who did not. *Gerontologist*, 1975, *15*, 350–356.

Brody, S. J., Poulshock, S. W., & Masciocchi, C. F. The family caring unit: A major consideration in the long-term support system. *Gerontologist*, 1978, *18*, 556–561.

Bultena, G. L., & Wood, V. The American retirement community: Bane or blessing? *Journal of Gerontology*, 1969, *24*, 209–217.

Burgess, E. W. *Aging in western societies*. Chicago: University of Chicago Press, 1960.

Burke, P. G., & Tully, J. C. The measurement of role identity. *Social Forces*, 1977, *55*, 881–897.

Burr, W. R. Satisfaction with various aspects of marriage over the life cycle: A random middle-class sample. *Journal of Marriage and the Family*, 1970, *32*, 29–37.

Butler, R. A. *Why survive? Being old in America*. New York: Harper & Row, 1975.

Campbell, A., Converse, P. E., & Rodgers, W. L. *The quality of American life*. New York: Russell Sage Foundation, 1976.

Carp, F. M. *A future for the aged*. Austin: University of Texas Press, 1966.

Carp, F. M. (Ed.). *Retirement*. New York: Behavioral Publications, 1972.

Carp, F. M. Long-range satisfaction with housing. *Gerontologist*, 1975a, *15*, 68–72.

Carp, F. M. Impact of improved housing on morale and life satisfaction. *Gerontologist*, 1975b, *15*, 511–515.

Carp, F. M. Impact of improved living environment on health and life expectancy. *Gerontologist*, 1977, *17*, 242–249.

Clayton, P. J., Halikas, J. A., Maurice, W. L., & Robins, E. Anticipatory grief and widowhood. *British Journal of Psychiatry*, 1973, *122*, 47–51.

Cleveland, W. P., & Gianturco, D. T. Remarriage probability after widowhood: A retrospective method. *Journal of Gerontology*, 1976, *31*, 99–103.

Coelho, G. V., Hamburg, D. A., & Adams, J. E. (Eds.). *Coping and adaptation*. New York: Basic Books, 1974.

Cottrell, F., & Atchley, R. C. *Women in retirement: A preliminary report*. Oxford, Ohio: Scripps Foundation, 1969.

Datan, N., & Ginsberg, L. H. (Eds.). *Life-span developmental psychology: Normative life crises*. New York: Academic Press, 1975.

Davidson, W. R., & Kunze, K. R. Psychological, social, and economic meanings of work in modern societies: Their effects on the worker facing retirement. *Gerontologist*, 1965, 5, 129–133.

de Charms, R. *Personal causations*. New York: Academic Press, 1968.

Deutscher, I. The quality of postparental life. In B. L. Neugarten (Ed.), *Middle age and aging*. Chicago: University of Chicago Press, 1968.

Eisdorfer, C. Adaptation to loss of work. In F. M. Carp (Ed.), *Retirement*. New York: Behavioral Publications, 1972.

Eisdorfer, C., & Lawton, M. P. (Eds.). *The psychology of adult development and aging*. Washington, D. C.: American Psychological Association, 1973.

Epstein, S. The self-concept revisited: Or a theory of a theory. *American Psychologist*, 1973, *28*, 404–416.

Eribes, R. A., & Bradley-Rawls, M. The underutilization of nursing home facilities by Mexican-American elderly in the Southwest. *Gerontologist*, 1978, *18*, 363–371.

Estes, C. L., & Freeman, H. C. Strategies of design and research for intervention. In R. H. Binstock & E. Shanas (Eds.), *Handbook of aging and the social sciences*. New York: Van Nostrand Reinhold, 1976.

Ezekiel, R. S. The personal future and Peace Corps competence. *Journal of Personality and Social Psychology*, 1968, *8*, Part II.

Ferrari, N. A. Freedom of choice. *Social Work*, 1963, *8*, 105–106.

Fillenbaum, G. G. On the relation between attitude to work and attitude to retirement. *Journal of Gerontology*, 1971, *24*, 244–248.

Fillenbaum, G. G. The longitudinal retirement history study: Methodological and substantive issues. *Gerontologist*, 1979, *19*, 203–209.

Fillenbaum, G. G., & Maddox, G. L. Work after retirement: An investigation into some psychologically relevant variables. *Gerontologist*, 1974, *14*, 418–424.

Fox, J. H. Effects of retirement and former work life on women's adaptation in old age. *Journal of Gerontology*, 1977, *32*, 196–202.

French, J. R. P., Jr., Rodgers, W., & Cobb, S. Adjustment as person-environment fit. In G. V. Coelho, D. A. Hamburg, & J. E. Adams (Eds.), *Coping and adaptation*. New York: Basic Books, 1974.

Friedmann, E., & Havighurst, R. J. *The meaning of work and retirement*. Chicago: University of Chicago Press, 1954.

Fritz, D. *The changing retirement scene*. Los Angeles: Andrus Gerontology Center, 1978.

George, L. K., & Maddox, G. L. Subjective adaptation to loss of the work role: A longitudinal study. *Journal of Gerontology*, 1977, 32, 456–462.

Gerber, I., Rusalem, R., Hannon, N., Battin, D., & Arkin, A. Anticipatory grief and aged widows and widowers. *Journal of Gerontology*, 1975, *30*, 225–229.

Gernant, L. What 814 retired professors say about retirement. *Gerontologist*, 1972, *12*, 349–353.

Glasmer, F. D., & DeJong, G. F. The efficacy of preretirement preparation programs for industrial workers. *Journal of Gerontology*, 1975, *30*, 595–600.

Glick, I. O., Weiss, R. D., & Parkes, C. M. *The first year of bereavement*. New York: Wiley, 1974.

Goffman, E. *The presentation of self in everyday life*. Garden City, New York: Doubleday, 1959.

Gordon, C., & Gergen, K. J. (Eds.). *The self in social interaction*. New York: Wiley, 1968.

Gordon, S. K., (Whitbourne) & Vinacke, W. E. Self and ideal self-concepts and dependency in aged persons residing in institutions. *Journal of Gerontology*, 1971, *26*, 337–345.

Goudy, W. J., Powers, E. A. & Keith, P. Work and retirement: A test of attitudinal relationship. *Journal of Gerontology*, 1975a, *30*, 193–198.

Goudy, W. J., Powers, E. A., & Keith, P. Work and retirement: A test of attitudinal relation-Profile examination. *Experimental Aging Research*, 1975b, *1*, 267–279.

Grinker, R. R., Sr. "Mentally healthy" young males (homoclites). *Archives of General Psychiatry*, 1962, *5*, 405–453.

Gutman, G. M., & Herbert, C. P. Mortality rates among relocated extended-care patients. *Journal of Gerontology*, 1976, *31*, 352–357.

Gutmann, D. Ego-psychological and developmental approaches to the "retirement crisis" in men. In F. M. Carp (Ed.), *Retirement*. New York: Behavioral Publications, 1972.

Haanes-Olsen, L. Lower pensionable age in Norway. *Social Security Bulletin*, 1974, *37*.

Hagestad, G. O. *Role change in adulthood: The transition to the empty nest*. Unpublished paper, 1977.

Hagestad, G. O., & Snow, R. B. *Young adult offspring as interpersonal resources in middle age*. Paper presented at annual meeting of the Gerontological Society, San Francisco, 1977.

Hamburg, D. A., Coelho, G. V., & Adams, J. E. Coping and adaptation: Steps toward a synthesis of biological and social perspectives. In G. V. Coelho, D. A. Hamburg, & J. E. Adams (Eds.), *Coping and adaptation*. New York: Basic Books, 1974.

Harkins, E. B. Effects of empty-nest transition on self-report of psychological and physical well-being. *Journal of Marriage and the Family*, 1978, *40*, 459–556.

Harris, L. *The myth and reality of aging in America*. Washington, D.C.: National Council on Aging, 1975.

Haynes, S. G., McMichael, A. J., & Tyroler, H. A. Survival after early and normal retirement. *Journal of Gerontology*, 1978, *33*, 269–278.

Hays, W. C., & Mindel, C. H. Extended kinship relations in Black and White families. *Journal of Marriage and the Family*, 1973, *35*, 51–57.

Hendricks, J., & Hendricks, C. D. *Aging in mass society*. Cambridge, Mass.: Winthrop Publishers, 1977.

Heyman, D. K., & Gianturco, D. T. Long-term adaptation by the elderly to bereavement. *Journal of Gerontology*, 1973, *28*, 350–362.

Hill, R. *Family development in three generations*. Cambridge, Mass.: Schenkman Publishing Co., 1970.

Hochschild, A. R. *The unexpected community*. Berkeley: University of California Press, 1973.

Holmes, T. H., & Rahe, R. H. The social readjustment rating scale. *Journal of Psychosomatic Research*, 1967, *11*, 213-218.

House, J. S. Occupational stress and coronary heart disease: A review and theoretical integration. *Journal of Health and Social Behavior*, 1974, *15*, 12–27.

Hudson, R. B. The "graying" of the federal budget and its consequences for old-age policy. *Gerontologist*, 1978, *18*, 428–440.

Ingram, D. K., & Barry, J. R. National statistics on deaths in nursing homes: Interpretations and implications. *Gerontologist*, 1977, *17*, 303–308.

Institute of Interdisciplinary Studies. *Indicators of the status of the elderly in the United States*. Washington, D. C.: U. S. Department of Health, Education, & Welfare, 1974.

Irelan, L. M., Motley, D. K., Schwab, K., Sherman, S. R., & Murray, J. *Almost 65: Baseline data from the retirement history study*. Washington D.C.: Social Security Administration, 1976.

Jahoda, M. *Current conceptions of positive mental health*. New York: Basic Books, 1958.

Janis, I. L. Vigilance and decision making in personal crises. In G. V. Coelho, D. A. Hamburg, & J. E. Adams (Eds.), *Coping and adaptation*. New York: Basic Books, 1974.

Jaslow, P. Employment, retirement, and morale among older women. *Journal of Gerontology*, 1976, *31*, 212–218.

Jasnau, K. F. Individualized versus mass transfer of nonpsychotic geriatric patients from mental hospitals to nursing homes, with special reference to death rate. *Journal of American Geriatric Society*, 1967, *15*, 280–284.

Johnson, L., & Strouther, G. B. Job expectations and retirement planning. *Journal of Gerontology*, 1962, *17*, 418–423.

Kaas, M. J. Sexual expression of the elderly in nursing homes. *Gerontologist*, 1978, *18*, 372–378.

Kalt, N. C., & Kohn, M. H. Pre-retirement counseling: Characteristics of programs and preferences of retirees. *Gerontologist*, 1975, *15*, 179–181.

Kasschau, P. L. Re-evaluating the need for retirement preparation programs. *Industrial Gerontology*, 1974, *1*, 42–59.

Kasteler, J., Gray, R., & Carruth, M. Involuntary relocation of the elderly. *Gerontologist*, 1968, *8*, 276–279.

Kastenbaum, R. S., & Candy, S. The 4% fallacy: A methodological and empirical critique of extended care facility program statistics. *International Journal of Aging and Human Development*, 1973, *4*, 15–21.

Kell, D., & Patton, C. V. Reaction to induced early retirement. *Gerontologist*, 1978, *18*, 173–180.

Kerckhoff, A. C. Norm-value clusters and the "strain toward consistency" among older married couples. In I. H. Simpson & J. C. McKinney (Eds.), *Social aspects of aging*. Durham, N. C.: Duke University Press, 1966.

Killian, E. Effects of geriatric transfers on mortality rates. *Social Work*, 1970, *15*, 19–26.

Kimmell, D. C., Price, K. F., & Walker, J. W. Retirement choice and retirement satisfaction. *Journal of Gerontology*, 1978, *33*, 575-585.

Kowalski, N. C. Fire at a home for the aged: A study of short-term mortality following dislocation of elderly residents. *Journal of Gerontology*, 1978, *33*, 601–602.

Kreps, J. M. *Lifetime allocation of work and leisure* (Social Security Administration Research Report No. 22). Washington, D.C.: Government Printing Office, 1968.

Kuhn, M. H., & McPartland, T. S. Empirical investigations of self-attitudes. *American Sociological Review*, 1954, *19*, 68–76.

Kuypers, J. A., & Bengtson, V. L. Social breakdown and competence. *Human Development*, 1973, *16*, 181–201.

Lakoff, S. A. The future of social intervention. In R. H. Binstock & E. Shanas (Eds.), *Handbook of aging and the social sciences*. New York: Van Nostrand Reinhold, 1976.

Lawton, M. P., Brody, E. M., & Turner-Massey, P. The relationship of environmental factors to changes in well-being. *Gerontologist*, 1978, *18*, 133–137.

Lawton, M. P., & Cohen, J. The generality of housing impact on the well-being of older people. *Journal of Gerontology*, 1974, *29*, 194–204.

Lawton, M.P., Nahemow, L., & Teaff, J. Housing characteristics and the well-being of elderly tenants in federally assisted housing. *Journal of Gerontology*, 1975, *30*, 601–607.

Lawton, M. P., Newcomer, R. J., & Byerts, T. O. (Eds.). *Community planning for an aging society: Designing services and facilities*. Stroudsberg, Penn: Dowden, Hutchinson, & Ross, 1976,

Lawton, M. P., & Yaffe, S. Mortality, morbidity, and voluntary change of residence by older people. *Journal of American Geriatrics Society*, 1970, *18*, 823–831.

Lazarus, R. S. *Psychological stress and the coping process*. New York: McGraw-Hill 1966.

Levinson, D. J. *The seasons of a man's life*. New York: Alfred A. Knopf, 1978.

Lieberman, M. A. Adaptive processes in late life. In N. Datan & L. H. Ginsberg (Eds.), *Life-span developmental psychology: Normative life crises*. New York: Academic Press, 1975.

Linton, R. *A study of man*. New York: Appleton-Century, 1936.

Lipman, A. Public housing and attitudinal adjustment in old age: A comparative study. *Journal of Geriatric Psychiatry*, 1968, *2*, 88–101.

Lopata, H. Z. Loneliness: Forms and components. *Social Problems*, 1969, *17*, 248–262.

Lopata, H. Z. *Widowhood in an American city*. Cambridge, Mass.: Schenkman Publishing Co., 1973a.

Lopata, H. Z. Self-identity in marriage and widowhood. *The Sociological Quarterly*, 1973b, *14*, 407–418.

Lowenthal, M. F. Intentionality: Toward a framework of the study of adaptation in adulthood. *Aging and Human Development*, 1971, *2*, 79–95.

Lowenthal, M. F., & Chiriboga, D. Transition to the empty nest: Crisis, challenge, or relief? *Archives of General Psychiatry*, 1972, *26*, 8–14.

Lowenthal, M. F., & Chiriboga, D. Social stress and adaptation: Toward a life course perspective. In C. Eisdorfer & M. P. Lawton (Eds.), *The psychology of adult development and aging*. Washington, D. C.: American Psychological Association, 1973.

Lowenthal, M. F., & Robinson, B. Social networks and isolation. In R. H. Binstock & E. Shanas (Eds.), *Handbook of aging and the social sciences*. New York: Van Nostrand Reinhold, 1976.

Lowenthal, M. F., Thurnher, M., & Chiriboga, D. *Four stages of life*. San Francisco: Jossey-Bass, 1975.

Maddison, D., & Viola, A. The health of widows in the year following bereavement. *Journal of Psychosomatic Research*, 1968, *12*, 297–306.

Maher, B. (Ed.). *Progress in experimental personality research* (Vol. 3). New York: Academic Press, 1966.

Markson, E., & Cummings, J. A strategy of necessary mass transfer and its impact on patient mortality. *Journal of Gerontology*, 1974, *29*, 315–321.

Marlowe, R. A. *When they closed the doors at Modesto*. Presented at National Institute of Mental Health Conference on the Closure of State Hospitals, 1974.

Marris, P. *Widows and their families*. London: Routledge & Kegan Paul, 1958.

McGrath, J. E. Major substantive issues: Time, setting, and the coping process. In J. E. McGrath (Ed.), *Social and psychological factors in stress*. New York: Holt, Rinehart & Winston, 1970a.

McGrath, J. E. Settings, measures, and themes: An integrative review of some research on social-psychological factors in stress. In J. E. McGrath (Ed.), *Social and Psychological factors in stress*. New York: Holt, Rinehart & Winston, 1970b.

McGrath, J. E. (Ed.). *Social and psychological factors in stress*. New York: Holt, Rinehart & Winston, 1970c.

McKain, W. C. *Retirement marriage*. Storrs, Connecticut: Storrs Agricultural Station, Monograph 3, 1969.

Mechanic, D. Some problems in developing a social psychology of adaptation to stress. In J. E. McGrath (Ed.), *Social and psychological factors in stress*. New York: Holt, Rinehart & Winston, 1970.

Mechanic, D. Social structure and personal adaptation: Some neglected dimensions. In G. V. Coelho, D. A. Hamburg, & J. E. Adams (Eds.), *Coping and adaptation*. New York: Basic Books, 1974.

References   *147*

Miller, D. B., & Beer, S. Patterns of friendship among patients in a nursing home setting. *Gerontologist*, 1977, *17*, 269–275.

Morgan, L. A. A re-examination of widowhood and morale. *Journal of Gerontology*, 1976, *31*, 687–695.

Morris, J. N. Changes in morale experienced by elderly institutional applicants along the institutional path. *Gerontologist*, 1975, *15*, 345–349.

Murdock, S. H., & Schwartz, D. F. Family structures and use of agency services: An examination of patterns among elderly native Americans. *Gerontologist*, 1978, *18*, 475–481.

National Center for Health Statistics, Health Resources Administration. Current Estimates from the Health Interview Survey: United States, 1977. *Vital and health statistics* (Series no. 126). Washington, D. C.: U. S. Government Printing Office, 1978.

Neugarten, B. L. (Ed.). *Personality in middle age and late life*. New York: Atherton, 1964.

Neugarten, B. L. (Ed.). *Middle age and aging*. Chicago: University of Chicago Press, 1968.

Neugarten, B. L., Crotty, W. J., & Tobin, S. S. Personality types in an aged population. In B. L. Neugarten (Ed.), *Personality in middle age and late life*. New York: Atherton, 1964.

Neugarten, B. L., Havighurst, R. J., & Tobin, S. S. Personality patterns of aging. In B. L. Neugarten (Ed.), *Middle age and aging*. Chicago: University of Chicago Press, 1968.

Neugarten, B. L., & Weinstein, K. K. The changing American grandparent. *Journal of Marriage and the Family*, 1964, *26*, 199–204.

Noelker, L., & Harel, Z. Predictors of well-being and survival among institutionalized aged. *Gerontologist*, 1978, *18*, 562–567.

Palmore, E. Differences in the retirement patterns of men and women. *Gerontologist*, 1965, *5*, 4–8.

Palmore, E. Total chance of institutionalization among the aged. *Gerontologist*, 1976, *16*, 504–507.

Parkes, C. M. *Bereavement: Studies of grief in adult life*. New York: International Universities Press, 1972.

Parnes, H. S., Adams, A. V., Andrisani, P., Kohen, A. I., & Nestel, G. *The pre-retirement years: Five years in the work lives of middle-aged men*. Columbus, Ohio: Center for Human Resources Research, 1974.

Pastalan, L. *Report on Pennsylvania nursing home relocation program: Interim research findings*. University of Michigan, Ann Arbor: Institute for Gerontology, 1976.

Pearlin, L. I., & Schooler, C. The structure of coping. *Journal of Health and Social Behavior*, 1978, *19*, 2–21.

Pino, C. J., Rosica, L. M., & Carter, T. J. The differential effects of relocation on nursing home patients. *Gerontologist*, 1978, *18*, 167–172.

Plonk, M. A., & Pulley, M. A. Financial management practices of retired couples. *Gerontologist*, 1977, *17*, 256–261.

Pollak, W. Utilization of alternative care settings by the elderly. In M. P. Lawton, R. J. Newcomer, & Byerts, T. O. (Eds.), *Community planning for an aging society: Designing services and facilities*. Stroudsberg, Penn.: Dowden, Hutchinson, & Ross, 1976.

Quinn, J. F. *Retirement patterns of self-employed workers*. Paper presented at conference on retirement policy and further population aging, Durham, 1978.

Rahe, R. H. Stress and strain in coronary heart disease. *Journal of the South Carolina Medical Association*, 1976, 7–14.

Rahe, R. G., Meyer, M., Smith, M., Kjaer, G., & Holmes, T. H. Social stress and illness onset. *Journal of Psychosomatic Research*, 1964, *8*, 35–44.

Reichard, S., Livson, F., & Peterson, P. G. *Aging and personality*. New York: Wiley, 1962.

Reid, D. W., Haas, G., & Hawkins, D. Locus of desired control and positive self-concept of the elderly. *Journal of Gerontology*, 1977, *32*, 441–450.

Robertson, J. F. Significance of grandparents: Perceptions of young adult grandchildren. *Gerontologist*, 1976, *16*, 137–140.

Robertson, J. F. Grandmotherhood: A study of role conceptions. *Journal of Marriage and the Family*, 1977, *38*, 165–174.

Rollins, B. C., & Feldman, H. Marital satisfaction over the family life cycle. *Journal of Marriage and the Family*, 1970, *32*, 20–28.

Rose, A. M. (Ed.). *Human behavior and social processes: An interactionist approach*. Boston: Houghton Mifflin, 1962.

Rosenmayr, L., & Köckeis, E. Propositions for a sociological theory of aging and the family. *International Social Science Journal,* 1963, *15,* 410–426.

Rosenberg, M. Psychological selectivity in self-esteem formation. In C. Gordon & K. J. Gergen (Eds.), *The self in social interaction.* New York: Wiley, 1968.

Rosow, I. Forms and functions of adult socialization. *Social Forces,* 1965, *44,* 35–45.

Rosow, I. *Social integration of the aged.* New York: Free Press, 1967.

Rosow, I. The social context of the aging self. *Gerontologist,* 1973, *13,* 82–87.

Rosow, I. *Socialization to old age.* Berkeley: University of California Press, 1974.

Rosow, I. Status and role change through the life span. In R. H. Binstock & E. Shanas (Eds.), *Handbook of aging and the social sciences.* New York: Van Nostrand Reinhold, 1976.

Rotter, J. B. Generalized expectancies for internal versus external control. *Psychological Monographs,* 1966, *80,* 1–28.

Rotter, J. B. A new scale for the measurement of interpersonal trust. *Journal of Personality,* 1967, *35,* 651–665.

Rotter, J. B. Some problems and misconceptions related to the construct of internal versus external control of reinforcement. *Journal of Consulting and Clinical Psychology,* 1975, *43,* 55–67.

Rowe, A. R. The retirement of academic scientists. *Journal of Gerontology,* 1972, *27,* 113–118.

Rulton, R. (Ed.). *Death and identity.* New York: Wiley, 1965.

Schoenberg, B., Gerber, I., Weiner, A., Kutscher, A. H., Peretz, D., & Carr, A (Eds.). *Psychosocial aspects of bereavement.* New York: Columbia University Press, 1975.

Schulz, R., & Brenner, G. Relocation of the aged: A review and theoretical analysis. *Journal of Gerontology,* 1977, *32,* 323–333.

Schwab, J. J., Chalmers, J. M., Conroy, S. J., Farris, P. B., & Markush, R. E. Studies in grief: A preliminary report. In B. Schoenberg, I. Gerber, A. Weiner, A. H. Kutscher, D. Peretz, & Carr, A. (Eds.), *Psychosocial aspects of bereavement.* New York: Columbia University Press, 1975.

Schwab, K. A. *Gradual retirement and adjustment in retirement.* Paper presented at annual meeting of the Gerontological Society, San Francisco, 1977.

Seltzer, M. M., & Atchley, R. C. The impact of structural integration into the profession on work commitment, potential for disengagement, and leisure preferences among social workers. *Sociological Focus,* 1971, *5,* 9–17.

Shanas, E. Health and adjustment in retirement. *Gerontologist,* 1970, *10,* 19–20.

Sheppard, H. L. Work and retirement. In R. H. Binstock & E. Shanas (Eds.), *Handbook of aging and the social sciences.* New York: Van Nostrand Reinhold, 1976.

Sheppard, H.L., & Philibert, M. Employment and retirement: Roles and activities. *Gerontologist,* 1972, *12,* 29–35.

Sherman S. R. Patterns of contacts for residents of age-segregated and age-integrated housing. *Journal of Gerontology,* 1975a, *30,* 103–107.

Sherman S. R. Mutual assistance and support in retirement housing. *Journal of Gerontology,* 1975b, *30,* 479–483.

Shrut, S. Attitudes toward old age and death. In R. Rulton (Ed.), *Death and identity.* New York: Wiley, 1965.

Simpson, I. H., Back, K. W., & McKinney, J. C. Attributes of work, involvement in society, and self-evaluation in retirement. In I. H. Simpson & J. C. McKinney (Eds.), *Social aspects of aging.* Durham, N. C.: Duke University Press, 1966a.

Simpson, I. H., Back, K. W., & McKinney, J. C. Orientation toward work and retirement and self-evaluation in retirement. In I. H. Simpson & J. C. McKinney (Eds.), *Social aspects of aging.* Durham, N. C.: Duke University Press, 1966b.

Simpson, I. H., Back, K. W., & McKinney, J. C. Exposure to information on, preparation for, and self-evaluation in retirement. In I. H. Simpson & J. C. McKinney (Eds.), *Social aspects of aging.* Durham, N. C.: Duke University Press, 1966c.

Simpson, I. H., & McKinney, J. C. (Eds.). *Social aspects of aging.* Durham, N. C.: Duke University Press, 1966.

Smith, M. B. Explorations in competence: A study of Peace Corps teachers in Ghana. *American Psychologist,* 1966, *21,* 556–566.

Soldo, B. J. Accounting for racial differences in institutional placements. Paper presented at annual meeting of the Gerontological Society, San Francisco, 1977.

Spasoff, R. A., Kraus, A. S., Beattie, E. J., Jolden, D. E. W., Lawson, J. S., Rodenburg, M., & Woodcock, G. M. A longitudinal study of elderly residents of long stay institutions: I. Early response to institutional care: II. The situation one year after admission. *Gerontologist*, 1978, *18*, 281–292.

Staats, S. Internal versus external locus of control for three age groups. *International Journal of Aging and Human Development*, 1974, *5*, 7–10.

Steiner, I. D. The resolution of interpersonal disagreements. In B. Maher (Ed.), *Progress in experimental personality research* (Vol. 3). New York: Academic Press, 1966.

Steiner, I. D. Strategies for controlling stress in interpersonal situations. In J. E. McGrath (Ed.), *Social and psychological factors in stress*. New York: Holt, Rinehart & Winston, 1970.

Steiner, I. D., & Johnson, H. H. Relationships among dissonance reducing responses. *Journal of Abnormal and Social Psychology*, 1964, *68*, 38–44.

Stokes, R. G., & Maddox, G. L. Some social factors in retirement adaptation. *Journal of Gerontology*, 1968, *22*, 329–333.

Storandt, M., & Wittels, I. Maintenance of function in relocation of community-dwelling older adults. *Journal of Gerontology*, 1975, *30*, 608–612.

Storandt, M., Wittels, I., & Botwinick, J. Predictors of a dimension of well-being in the relocated healthy aged. *Journal of Gerontology*, 1975, *30*, 97–102.

Streib, G. F. Social stratification and aging. In R. H. Binstock & E. Shanas (Eds.), *Handbook of aging and the social sciences*. New York: Van Nostrand Reinhold, 1976.

Streib, G. F., & Schneider, C. H. *Retirement in American society*. Ithaca, N. Y.: Cornell University Press, 1971.

Sussman, M. B. The family life of older people. In R. H. Binstock & E. Shanas (Eds.), *Handbook of aging and the social sciences*. New York: Van Nostrand Reinhold, 1976.

Teaff, J. D., Lawton, M. P., Nahemow, L., & Carlson, D. Impact of age integration on the well-being of elderly tenants in public housing. *Journal of Gerontology*, 1978, *33*, 130–133.

Terkel, S. *Working*. New York: Random House, 1972.

Thompson, W. E., Streib, G. F., & Kosa, J. The effect of retirement on personal adjustment: A panel analysis. *Journal of Gerontology*, 1960, *15*, 165–169.

Tibbits, C. T. (Ed.). *Handbook of social gerontology*. Chicago: University of Chicago Press, 1960.

Tobin, S. S., & Lieberman, M. A. *Last home for the aged*. San Francisco: Jossey-Bass, 1976.

Treas, J., & Van Helst, A. Marriage and remarriage rates among older Americans. *Gerontologist*, 1976, *16*, 132–136.

Troll, L. E. The family of later life: A decade review. *Journal of Marriage and the Family*, 1971, *33*, 263–290.

Turner, R. H. Role-taking, role standpoint, and reference group behavior. *American Journal of Sociology*, 1956, *61*, 316–328.

Turner, R. H. Role-taking: Process versus conformity. In A. M. Rose (Ed.), *Human behavior and social processes: An interactionist approach*. Boston: Houghton Mifflin, 1962.

Tyler, F. B. Individual psychosocial competence: A personality configuration. *Educational and Psychological Measurement*, 1978, *38*, 309–323.

U. S. Bureau of the Census. *Consumer income reports, current population surveys* (Series P–60, No. 59). Washington, D.C.: U.S. Government Printing Office, April 1968.

U. S. Bureau of the Census. *Consumer income reports, current population surveys* (Series P–60, No. 90). Washington, D. C.: U. S. Government Printing Office, December, 1973.

U. S. Bureau of the Census. *Current population reports* (Series P–20, No. 287). Washington, D. C.: U.S. Government Printing Office, 1975.

U.S. Bureau of the Census. *Geographic mobility of Americans: An international comparison* (Series P–23, No. 64). Washington, D.C.: U.S. Government Printing Office, 1976.

U. S. Bureau of the Census. *Consumer income reports, current population surveys* (Series P–60, No. 116). Washington, D. C.: U. S. Government Printing Office, July, 1978.

U. S. Department of Health, Education and Welfare. *Limitation of activity due to chronic conditions* (Public Health Service, Series 10). Washington, D.C.: U.S. Government Printing Office, 1972.

Vinick, B. H. Remarriage in old age. *The Family Coordinator*, 1978, *27*, 359–363.

Wang, G. C. Flexible retirement feature of German pension reform. *Social Security Bulletin*, 1973, *35*.

Warheit, G. J., Holzer, C. E., III, Bell, R. A., & Arey, S. A. Sex, marital status, and mental health: A reappraisal. *Social Forces,* 1976, *55,* 459–470.

Weber, M. *The Protestant ethic and the spirit of capitalism.* New York: Charles Scribner's Sons, 1958.

White, R. W. Strategies of adaptation: An attempt at systematic description. In G. V. Coelho, D. A. Hamburg, & J. E. Adams (Eds.), *Coping and adaptation.* New York: Basic Books, 1974.

Wittels, I., & Botwinick, J. Survival in relocation. *Journal of Gerontology,* 1974, *29,* 440–443.

Wolk, S., & Telleen, S. Psychological and social correlates of life satisfaction as a function of residential constraint. *Journal of Gerontology,* 1976, *31,* 89–98.

Wright, J. D., & Hamilton, F. R. Work satisfaction and age: Some evidence for the "job change" hypothesis. *Social Forces,* 1978, *56,* 1140–1158.

Zweig, J., & Csank, J. Effects of relocation on chronically ill geriatric patients of a medical unit: Mortality rates. *Journal of American Geriatrics Society,* 1975, *23,* 132–136.

Name Index

deCharms, R., 144
De Jong, G. F., 69, 145
Deutscher, I., 83, 144

Eisdorfer, C., 65, 144, 147
Epstein, S., 15, 144
Eribes, R. A., 114, 144
Estes, C. L., 135, 136, 144
Ezekiel, R. S., 33, 145

Farris, P. B., 95, 149
Feldman, H., 80–84, 148
Ferrari, N. A., 117, 120, 145
Fillenbaum, G. G., 59, 60, 61, 76, 145
Fox, J. H., 64, 65, 145
Freeman, H. C., 135, 136, 144
French, J. R. P., 30, 145
Friedmann, E., 59, 60, 63, 145
Fritz, D., 67, 145

George, L. K., 61, 64, 65, 71, 145
Gerber, I., 95, 145, 149
Gergen, K. J., 145, 149
Gernant, L., 60, 145
Gianturco, D. T., 92, 93, 144, 146
Ginsberg, L. H., 144, 147
Glasmer, F. D., 69, 145
Glick, I. O., 89–98, 100–101, 145
Goffman, E., 17, 145
Gordon, C., 145, 149
Gordon, S. K., 118, 145
Goudy, W. J., 59, 60, 145
Grad, S., 75–76
Gray, R., 106, 110, 146
Grinker, R. R., 32, 145
Guptill, C. S., 61, 143
Gutman, G. M., 117, 145
Gutmann, D., 66–67, 145

Haanes-Olsen, L., 75, 145
Haas, G., 34, 148
Hagestad, G. O., 80, 83–84, 145
Halikas, J. A., 95, 143, 144
Hamburg, D. A., 32, 144, 145, 146, 147, 151
Hamilton, F. R., 59, 151
Hannon, N., 95, 145
Harel, Z., 119, 148
Harkins, E. B., 83–84, 145
Harris, L., 67–68, 74, 115, 134, 145
Havighurst, R. J., 34, 59, 60, 63, 145, 148
Hawkins, D., 34, 148
Haynes, S. G., 65, 145
Hays, W. C., 80, 145
Hendricks, C. D., 28, 78, 145
Hendricks, J., 28, 78, 145
Herbert, C. P., 117, 145
Heyman, D. K., 92, 146

Hill, R., 78, 146
Hochschild, A. R., 108, 109, 146
Holden, D. E. W., 116, 122, 150
Holmes, T. H., 9, 10, 146, 148
Holzer, C. E., 91, 151
House, J. S., 10, 50–54, 146
Hudson, R. B., 134, 146

Ingram, D. K., 112, 114, 146
Irelan, L. M., 64, 71, 146

Jahoda, M., 32, 33, 146
Janis, I. L., 31, 146
Jaslow, P., 64, 146
Jasnau, K. F., 120, 146
Johnson, H. H., 31, 150
Johnson, L., 60, 146

Kaas, M. J., 118, 146
Kalt, N. C., 67, 146
Kasschau, P. L., 67, 69, 146
Kasteler, J., 106, 110, 146
Kastenbaum, R. S., 114, 146
Keith, P., 59, 60, 145
Kell, D., 60, 61, 65, 146
Kerckhoff, A. C., 80, 146
Killian, E., 117, 146
Kimmel, D. C., 60, 146
Kjaer, G., 9, 148
Kleban, M. H., 106, 144
Köckeis, E., 79, 149
Kohen, A. I., 65, 148
Kohn, M. H., 67, 146
Kosa, J., 60, 61, 65, 150
Kowalski, N. C., 117, 146
Kraus, A. S., 116, 122, 150
Kreps, J. M., 75, 146
Kuhn, M. H., 16, 146
Kunze, K. R., 67, 144
Kutscher, A. H., 149
Kuypers, J. A., 38, 41–43, 146

Lakoff, S. A., 134, 136–137, 146
Lawson, J. S., 116, 122, 150
Lawton, M. P., 106, 108, 109, 110, 144, 146, 147, 148, 150
Lazarus, R. S., 27, 31, 32, 33, 147
Levin, M. A., 134, 135–136, 143
Levinson, D. J., 80, 147
Lieberman, M. A., 38–41, 114, 116–120, 122–124, 147, 150
Liebowitz, B., 106, 144
Linton, R., 2, 147
Lipman, A., 106, 147
Livson, F., 34, 66, 148
Lopata, H. Z., 88–98, 100–101, 147
Lowenthal, M. F., 10, 11, 29, 38, 47–50, 84, 147

Subject Index